...world's longest established
...brands,
...travel.

For more than 135 years our
guidebooks have unlocked the secrets
of destinations around the world,
sharing with travellers a wealth of
experience and a passion for travel.

**Rely on Thomas Cook as your
travelling companion on your next trip
and benefit from our unique heritage.**

Thomas Cook **pocket** guides

BOLOGNA

Thomas
Cook

Your travelling companion since 1873

Written by Zoë Ross with assistance from Fran Folsom
Updated by John Bleasdale

Published by Thomas Cook Publishing
A division of Thomas Cook Tour Operations Limited
Company registration no. 3772199 England
The Thomas Cook Business Park, 9 Coningsby Road,
Peterborough PE3 8SB, United Kingdom
Email: books@thomascook.com, Tel: +44 (0) 1733 416477
www.thomascookpublishing.com

Produced by Cambridge Publishing Management Limited
Burr Elm Court, Main Street, Caldecote CB23 7NU
www.cambridgepm.co.uk

ISBN: 978-1-84848-349-1

© 2007, 2009 Thomas Cook Publishing
This third edition © 2011
Text © Thomas Cook Publishing
Maps © Thomas Cook Publishing/PCGraphics (UK) Limited
Transport map © Communicarta Limited

Series Editor: Karen Beaulah
Production/DTP: Steven Collins

Printed and bound in Spain by GraphyCems

Cover photography © John Ferro Sims/Alamy

Although every care has been taken in compiling this publication, and the contents
are believed to be correct at the time of printing, Thomas Cook Tour Operations
Limited cannot accept any responsibility for errors or omission, however caused,
or for changes in details given in the guidebook, or for the consequences of any
reliance on the information provided. Descriptions and assessments are based on
the author's views and experiences when writing and do not necessarily represent
those of Thomas Cook Tour Operations Limited.

CONTENTS

SYMBOLS KEY

The following symbols are used throughout this book:

ⓐ address ☏ telephone ⓦ website address ⓔ email
🕐 opening times Ⓝ public transport connections ❶ important

The following symbols are used on the maps:

𝑖 information office		▪	point of interest
✈ airport		⭕	city
➕ hospital		⭕	large town
🛡 police station		○	small town
🚍 bus station		═	motorway
🚆 railway station		—	main road
✝ cathedral		—	minor road
❶ numbers denote featured		—	railway
cafés & restaurants			

Hotels and restaurants are graded by approximate price as follows:
£ budget price **££** mid-range price **£££** expensive

◗ *'Bologna la Rossa' – the red-hued city*

INTRODUCING
Bologna

Introduction

Emilia-Romagna, the heartland of northern Italy, has always played second fiddle to its neighbour Tuscany, which has long attracted tourists because of the treasures of Florence, Siena and Pisa. But Bologna, the capital of the region, is one of the most refined and enticing cities in the country, a fact that more people are beginning to discover as low-cost airlines head there. What's more, it has considerably fewer crowds.

Before being controlled by the papacy, and then brought under Italian Unification, the region was ruled by a range of powerful and wealthy aristocratic dynasties – the d'Este family in Ferrara and Modena, the Farnese in Parma, the Bentivoglios in Bologna and lesser dynasties in Ravenna and Rimini. Their legacies can still be seen in the many surviving magnificent Renaissance courts, castles and fortresses, as well as a few remaining towers that indicated their importance.

Bologna is also a city of *portici* (porticoes or arcades). Reportedly there are over 60 km (40 miles) of these covered walkways, which allow business, shopping and socialising to be carried out in all weathers in the historic centre, providing shade during the torrid summers and shelter during the rainy winters.

Bologna's *centro storico* (historic centre) has been recognised as the largest intact historical urban core in the world, and it is possible to admire important structures from the Roman period, remnants of the original medieval walls that used to surround the city, as well as vaults, arches and corbels from the 12th and 14th centuries.

But it is the city's reputation as a home to freethinkers that really established its fame. It is known, among other things, as *Bologna la Dotta* (the Learned), as its university, established in the 11th century, is the oldest in Europe. *Bologna la Rossa* (the Red) was a phrase originally coined to describe the red-hued buildings of the city, but was also reckoned to refer to the Communist tendencies of those living in the region. *Bologna la Grassa* (the Fat) is equally fitting. Food is sacred to the Bolognese, and the region's cuisine is respected throughout the country. That is hardly surprising when the region has produced some of Italy's most famous gastronomic delights, including Parmesan cheese, Parma ham and lasagne.

Away from the city, the poplar-studded landscape starts at the foothills of the Apennine mountains in the south and extends to the northern plain, the Pianura Padana. This has been a wheat-growing area since Roman times, and today its industry and agricultural businesses are Italy's most prosperous, making Emilia-Romagna one of the richest regions in Italy. This, in turn, lends Bologna and the whole area a sophisticated air – expect locals to be both well dressed and well mannered.

Cutting through the middle of the region, the Via Emilia (or A1 and A14) is a Roman military road constructed in 187 BC as part of the pilgrims' route to Rome and the way east to Ravenna and Venice. The towns that developed along the Via Emilia – including Piacenza and Modena – are some of Italy's most dramatic. Other towns easily accessible from Bologna are Parma, a wealthy provincial town famous for its architecture, Ferrara, which has an important Renaissance centre, and Ravenna, where you will find the world's best-preserved Byzantine mosaics. With the recent development of the high-speed train links provided by the Frecciarossa and Frecciaargento trains, many important centres in Italy are easily accessible from Bologna for day trips. Milan is only one hour away, Venice an hour and a half, and Florence only forty minutes. Even the journey to Napoli has been reduced to less than four hours. In this way Bologna has become a perfect central point for exploring all of Italy as well as a city well worth visiting in itself.

When to go

Unlike many destinations, there are no hard-and-fast rules about when to plan a visit to Bologna – each season offers something different. The one thing that is consistent is the warm welcome you'll receive from the local people.

SEASONS & CLIMATE

The months of July and, in particular, August can be uncomfortably hot; during the latter many locals head to the mountains or the coast, leaving some shops and restaurants closed for the entire month. The city is at its most crowded during Christmas, Easter and the Celebrazioni Madonna di San Luca in May (see page 10), but it's also at its most vibrant, so if you don't mind the throng these can be wonderful times to visit. To get the best out of the city, however, without excessive heat or crowds, aim to visit in spring or autumn. During March and April, and September and October, the air is warm, with an average temperature of 17°C (63°F), the skies are (usually) blue and the flowers in bloom. If you do visit in summer, make sure you wear lightweight fabrics such as cotton or linen, a hat and sun-block, and rehydrate regularly with bottled water. Italians take their midday siesta seriously for a reason – between 12.00 and 15.00 the heat is intense, so if you don't want to waste time sleeping, use this time to visit shady museums or churches (if they are open). Sturdy walking shoes are advisable at any time of year as the flagstoned streets can be unforgiving on high heels or lightweight soles.

ANNUAL EVENTS

There are literally hundreds of festivals year-round throughout the Emilia-Romagna region, and some of the most enjoyable are the smaller local affairs rather than flashy national events. Below are some of the highlights, but it's always best to check with local tourist offices about what's going on during your visit, as many dates are liable to change from year to year. Like all Italians, the Bolognese take their festivals very seriously, and a large part of the annual activities have their roots in the Catholic faith that's still so central to the country. Christmas, and in particular Holy Week – the run-up to Easter – are huge events, as is the February Carnival marking the start of Lent.

Particular to the region in this gastronomic heartland is the emphasis on food; almost every festival in and around Bologna will be accompanied by vast displays of local delicacies to be enjoyed by all.

January
Artefiera This internationally renowned modern and contemporary art fair sees museums in the city holding special exhibitions and conferences. Ⓦ www.artefiera.bolognafiere.it Ⓛ Late Jan

January & February
Future Film Festival If you're interested in cinema, the biggest names in new technology often feature at this important international festival, which showcases the digital technology that is increasingly used in today's films. Ⓐ Via del Pratello 21/2 Ⓣ 051 296 0672 Ⓦ www.futurefilmfestival.org

February & March
Carnival Italy tends to let the good times roll around Lent. The Emilia-Romagna region's festivals add their own local spice: **Festival of Sant' Apollonia** Ⓐ Bellaria-Igea Marina Ⓦ www.comune.bellaria-igea-marina.rn.it

Mardi Gras Carnival ⓐ Borgo Tossignano
ⓦ www.comune.borgotossignano.bo.it
Carnival San Giovanni (Shrove Tuesday) ⓐ Persiceto
ⓦ www.carnevalepersiceto

March
Sagra del Raviolo (Ravioli Festival) ⓐ Casalfiumanese
ⓦ www.comunedicasalfiumanese.it ⓛ Mid-Mar
Fiera del Bue Grasso (Festival of the Fat Ox) A cattle and folk-craft fair
that goes back centuries. ⓐ Cavriago ⓦ www.comune.cavriago.re.it
ⓛ Last weekend Mar

April & May
Formula 1 Grand Prix of San Marino The glitz, the glamour and
the burning rubber make this well worth a pit stop. ⓐ Imola
ⓦ www.formula1.com ⓛ Late Apr–early May

May
Celebrazioni Madonna di San Luca (also known as Festa di San Luca)
Ascension Day sees an effigy of the Virgin being conveyed to
Bologna from the Santuario di San Luca. ⓐ Between San
Pietro Cathedral, historical centre and Basilica di San Petronio
ⓛ Sat before the fifth Sun after Easter, and the following Wed
and Sun
Sposalizio del Mare (Espousal of the Sea) With knees-ups and a
regatta, this celebration has been taking place annually since 1445.
ⓐ Cervia ⓛ First weekend May

June
Palio delle Contrade An annual bash for a wedding of significance
that took place 500 years ago (see page 14).

Palio del Niballo A festival of ye olde worlde-style equestrianism, executed with a flourish. ❷ Faenza Ⓦ www.paliodifaenza.it
Ⓛ First week June

June & July
Ravenna Music Festival Local churches make a beautiful setting for opera, ballet and recitals. Ⓦ www.ravennafestival.org

⬥ *Maybe plan your trip to coincide with a local* palio *(see page 14)*

July

Feste Rinascimentali (Renaissance Festival) The entire town takes part in this festival, as over 400 local citizens flounce through the streets in period costume and restaurants organise meals based around Renaissance-era recipes. Ⓦ www.casteldelrio.provincia.bologna.it

August

Assumption of the Blessed Virgin Mary A big day in the Catholic calendar that sees celebrations everywhere. 🕒 15 Aug

September

La Città del Cibo (Bologna City of Food) For three days the streets and *piazze* of Bologna's centre fill with vendors selling local specialities, including tortellini and Parma ham. Free samples abound. Ⓦ www.bolognalacittadelcibo.it

Festival del Prosciutto di Parma (Parma Ham Festival) Although centred around Langhirano (home of the Museo del Prosciutto, or Parma Ham Museum), events also take place in 11 other towns in the region. It's also possible to visit *prosciutto* producers to see how this delicacy is made. Ⓦ www.festivaldelprosciuttodiparma.com 🕒 First two weeks Sept

September & October

Bologna Festival Classical music festival held at various locations throughout the city. Ⓦ www.bolognafestival.it

October

Ravenna Jazz Festival Three-day festival that started in 1974 with a Charles Mingus jazz workshop. Over the years it has hosted the Stan Getz Quartet and Herbie Hancock, among other jazz greats. Ⓦ www.erjn.it/ravenna 🕒 Last weekend Oct

October & November
Fiera Nazionale del Tartufo Nero di Fragno (National Truffle Festival)
Truffle tasting, truffle markets and 'truffle trail running', a race through truffle territory that's not for the faint of heart. ⓐ Calestano, Parma ⓦ www.tartufonerofragno.it ⓒ Sun, mid-Oct–mid-Nov

December
As the festive season approaches, most villages and towns construct exquisite Nativity scenes and organise sumptuous Christmas markets.
Bologna Motor Show As the original home of Ducati, Lamborghini and Maserati, it's no surprise that Bologna stages a Motor Show that draws international crowds by the thousands. Meet Formula 1 stars, check out new models or test-drive racing cars. ⓦ www.motorshow.it
ⓒ Mid-Dec

PUBLIC HOLIDAYS
Capodanno (New Year's Day) 1 Jan
La Befana (Epiphany) 6 Jan
Pasqua & Lunedi di Pasqua (Easter Sunday & Monday)
24 & 25 Apr 2011; 8 & 9 Apr 2012; 31 March & 1 Apr 2013
Festa della Liberazione (Liberation Day) 25 Apr
Festa del Lavoro (Labour Day) 1 May
Festa della Repubblica (Anniversary of the Republic) 2 June
Ferragosto (Feast of the Assumption) 15 Aug
San Petronio (Feast of Saint Petronio, Bologna's patron saint) 4 Oct
Tutti Santi (All Saints' Day) 1 Nov
Festa dell'Immacolata (Feast of the Immaculate Conception) 8 Dec
Natale (Christmas) 25 Dec
San Stefano (Boxing Day) 26 Dec

Palios

Palios, or, in Italian, *palii* (bareback horse races), have been a feature of the northern Italian landscape since medieval times, when the troubled relations between different districts meant that the military needed to keep their equestrian skills up to scratch. The races, therefore, were created as much for serious practical reasons as they were for showmanship and local pride.

Italy's most famous *palio* takes place in Siena in Tuscany, but the Emilia-Romagna region has more than its fair share of races to entertain the crowds. One of the best is also the oldest in Italy – the Palio di San Giorgio in Ferrara, which takes place either on the last Sunday in May or the first Sunday in June. Riders dressed in medieval costume and representing each of the eight districts (known as *contrade*) gallop through the city streets. All are vying for the *palio*, a brightly coloured flag that is the coveted first prize. It's a high-octane event, with the pavements lined with cheering supporters waving the flag that represents 'their' district. Aside from the race itself, there are plenty of other festivities, most of them continuing with the medieval pageantry theme.

On the first Sunday in June, the Palio delle Contrade takes place in San Secondo, just outside Parma, to commemorate the wedding, in 1523, of Pietro Maria Rossi III to Camilla Gonzaga of Mantova. The wedding was important: the bride and bridegroom came from two of the region's aristocratic families, which are still in existence today. The race culminates with a sumptuous banquet and a parade with thousands of people waving flags and wending their way through the streets of the town.

Although these races are firmly rooted in their medieval traditions, today they are also an excuse for partying, socialising and a bit of fun. Besides the main event there will often be more light-hearted competitions, such as a *palio* on donkeys, and girls' and boys' races.

▲ *The excitement of the* palio

History

The first settlers of northern and central Italy were the Etruscans; under the name Felsina, they founded the city that is now Bologna. They made much use of its strategic position, set as it is between the Mediterranean and Adriatic sea trading routes, as well as of its strong agricultural potential. But within just a few centuries the mighty power of the Roman Empire swept over the entire country and the Etruscan kings were no more. In the second century BC the Romans named the city Bononia (pronounced Bologna in local dialect), and in time it grew in both size and wealth, eventually becoming the most important city in Italy after Rome. After the fall of Rome, the landscape was ripe for new invaders, and in the 8th century the Lombards, moving south from what is now Germany and Austria, began to control much of the peninsula, including Bologna. Along with other cities such as Milan, Verona and Parma, Bologna joined the Lombard League, set up to protect themselves against the advances of the Holy Roman Empire. As such they became city-states, with a relative degree of governmental autonomy.

The Lombards believed in culture as a route to wealth and success, and undoubtedly one of the most important events in Bologna's history was the establishment of a university in 1088 – it is the oldest in Europe. Bologna soon became renowned as a city of enlightenment and education, which in turn brought it much wealth and reputation. The great poets Dante and Petrarch are among those who could name the university as their *alma mater*. The Middle Ages were, in fact, the city's Golden Age, during which time the porticoed arcades, towers and churches were constructed, largely financed by the great families of the time such as the Bentivoglio and the Farnese. At this time much of Italy was also engaged in the battle for supremacy being waged between the Papal States and the Holy Roman Empire, which were both vying for overall control. While these powers were caught up in political machinations, the Lombards were able to concentrate on their own cities, thus developing them into far more important and successful centres. By the 16th century, however, Bologna also became a Papal State, ruled from Rome, although in reality much of the governance was still controlled by the various aristocratic families that exercised considerable power over the region. Nevertheless, this was also another flourishing time for the city, particularly with the establishment of the Bolognese School, an art movement that saw the rise of the great Baroque artists such as Carracci, Domenichino and Guercino, whose works can now be seen in the Pinacoteca Nazionale (see page 88).

Papal rule was abandoned when Napoleon conquered Italy in 1800, but this was also the dawning of a new age. The Italians, having been ruled at various times by Greeks, Germans, Spaniards and now French, were tired of being governed by foreigners, and were equally not keen to return to Vatican rule. This gave rise to the *Risorgimento*, the political and social movement for a unified Italy. Bologna joined this campaign, becoming part of the Kingdom of Italy in 1859.

From that point until the present day Bologna has retained its top-draw reputation. Indeed, being selected as a European Capital of Culture in 2000 encouraged Bologna to strut its stuff in a big way, giving the rest of the world full exposure to its charms. Bologna also produced the man who was largely responsible for Italy's entry into the Eurozone, Romano Prodi. An influential European Commissioner, Prodi has also twice been Prime Minister of Italy, the only politician to have beaten the ubiquitous Silvio Berlusconi at the ballot box.

Lifestyle

*'I long for Bologna... where the foreigners are overwhelmed by
the warm welcome they are accorded... in Bologna everything
is beautiful, in both the material and moral sense... believe me,
you really do encounter good-hearted people, they are everywhere.'*
Giacomo Leopardi, poet and philosopher (1798–1837)

La Dotta, *La Grassa* and *La Rossa* (the Learned, the Fat and the
Red) are Bologna's nicknames, but it is an insistence on plain truth
that sets the Bolognese apart. In the 11th century it was the desire
for truth and law that led to the founding of the University of
Bologna. And it's the honest ingredients in the kitchen that have
made Bolognese food and cuisine among the best in Italy, and the
source of one of those nicknames. As for *La Rossa*, Bologna may be
full of socialist virtue (its municipal government was long in the
hands of the Italian Communist Party, now the PDS), but the city is
also very wealthy. *La Rossa* also refers to the typically red-coloured
stucco of the city's buildings.

Even its automotive industry is classy, with the likes of Lamborghini
and Ducati (motorcycles) headquartered here, and Maserati only
recently moved to nearby Modena. Its political energy is fuelled by
the 100,000 students living here, who give the city the air of a giant
university campus, especially in good weather, when they fill the
cafés and bars in every street and piazza.

For all Bologna's richly decorated churches, you'd hardly call it
a pious city. Between the freethinking students and the leftward
lean of its residents, the church is less of a dominating force here
than elsewhere in Italy. Even the city's cultural offerings reflect its
heady mix of tastes and styles, with everything from rap to jazz to

Renaissance madrigals, as well as avant-garde ballet, theatre and art exhibitions on offer at almost any time of year.

Even in August, when Italy's month-long holidays empty the city as though someone had pulled the plug, enough students remain to keep the *centro storico* lively. Though hip hop and grunge may have replaced the more sedate strains of early 19th-century music, Giacomo Leopardi would still recognise the city.

◯ *Fresh good food is very important to the Bolognese*

Culture

When Bologna was named European Capital of Culture in 2000, it marked a much-needed turnaround in the attention that the city received. Long in the shadow of Rome, Florence, Venice and Milan, Bologna was seen as something of a backwater, but this in fact belies a cultural tradition that dates back to the 11th century. The turn of the millennium, therefore, brought about a renaissance in the city's popularity and reputation.

The city has strong musical connections – Mozart, Rossini, Verdi and Wagner have all performed or staged their works here over the centuries. And the annual calendar of the entire region is still littered with a range of classical, jazz and other music events that are staged in both large, tailor-made venues and in more intimate church settings (see page 104). One of the highlights of the year is the annual opera season from November to June.

In terms of art and architecture, there have been several major contributors to the cultural landscape around the region. The most famous members of the 16th-century Bolognese School of art are the Carracci brothers and Guercino. In the same period the Flemish-born sculptor Giambologna earned his name from his incredible first commission, the Fontana del Nettuno in Piazza Maggiore (see page 69). Much of the area's landscape also owes itself to the great ruling families of the past, such as the Bentivoglio and the d'Este, who commissioned vast *palazzi* and looming towers to illustrate their importance to lesser citizens. Important artworks are housed together in the Pinacoteca Nazionale (see page 88) but, as in most of Italy, the majority of art treasures are still to be found in churches and cathedrals.

Piazza Maggiore often vibrates with the sound of a music festival

GIORGIO MORANDI

Giorgio Morandi was born in Bologna in 1890 and spent most of his life painting there or in the village of Vergato, 40 km (25 miles) from the city. His landscapes have been compared to the work of Cézanne for the recurring presence of similarly angular shapes and soft hues. Painting during a period of immense social upheaval, technological innovation and artistic expression, he was initially drawn to the work of the Futurists and Cubists. But ultimately he found his niche in more metaphysical painting, aligning himself with the artists Carra and De Chirico. He became the artist of simple, everyday objects – vases, fruit, windows – discovering them as if for the first time, revealing their hidden depths and imbuing them with an existential significance. Explaining his view that nothing is more abstract than reality, he once said, 'Everything is a mystery, ourselves and the most simple, most infinitesimal of things.'

In terms of literature, Bologna has never witnessed a great outpouring of prose or poetry as has, say, Florence or Venice, although nearby Ravenna is the burial place of Italy's greatest literary Titan, Dante, after he was banned from Florence (see page 126). The city's best-known modern-day author is Umberto Eco, whose acclaimed works include *The Name of the Rose* (1983) (later a successful film) and *Foucault's Pendulum* (1989). More recently Bologna has become the home of Luther Blissett and the Wu Ming Collective, a group of authors who have collaborated on novels such as *Q* and *'54*, to great international acclaim.

▶ *The Fontana del Nettuno and the Palazzo del Podesta*

MAKING THE MOST OF
Bologna

Shopping

The northern Italian cities are synonymous with style – and Bologna is no exception. If you crave designer gear, or just want to window-shop and soak up the glamour, head for the intersections of Via dell'Indipendenza, Via Ugo Bassi, Via Rizzoli and Via D'Azeglio, off Piazza Maggiore. These four streets are home to the big names, including Versace and Gucci. Via D'Azeglio is also one of the best places in the city for jewellery. Do note that Italy is well known for its leather goods: handbags, belts and shoes can be good value compared to prices in other countries.

One of the joys of the region is its street markets. Each day in spring and autumn there is a book market in Piazza XX Settembre, which is a magnet for bibliophiles. There are three flea markets of note that sell a variety of bric-a-brac, second-hand clothes and all manner of other goods. The Mercato di Antiquario on Via Santo Stefano (every second weekend of the month from September to June) is good for antiques; alternatively, try the weekend market, La Piazzola, in the Parco della Montagnola, or Mercato del Collezionismo, the collectors' market – every Thursday – on Piazza VIII Agosto (see page 84).

Bologna is a renowned centre of gastronomy, and all over the city you'll find mouthwatering cakes at *pasticcerie* (pastry shops), local wines at any *enoteca* and fresh bread at a *forno*. Don't forget to pick up some Parma ham and Parmesan cheese. Modena's balsamic vinegar is considered among the best in the world and makes an ideal souvenir. There are plenty of fabulous food markets, too. Mercato delle Urbe is on Via Ugo Bassi 2 and Mercato Orefici on Via dei Orefici. Both are open daily in the morning.

For a really beautiful and traditional souvenir, head out of the city to Faenza, 50 km (30 miles) southeast of Bologna. The town is

USEFUL SHOPPING PHRASES

What time do the shops open/close?
A che ora aprono/chiudono i negozi?
Ah keh ohrah ahprohnoh/kewdohnoh ee nehgotsee?

How much is this?
Quanto costa questo?
Kwantoh kostah kwestoh?

Can I try this on?
Posso provarlo?
Pohsoh prohvarloh?

My size is ...
La mia taglia è ...
Lah meeyah tahlyah eh ...

I'll take this one, thank you
Prenderò questo, grazie
Prehndehroh kwestoh, grahtsyeh

Can you show me the one in the window/this one?
Può mostrarmi quello in vetrina/questo?
Poh mohstrahrmee kwehloh een vehtreenah/kwestoh?

This is too large/too small/too expensive
Questo è troppo grande/troppo piccolo/troppo caro
Kwestoh eh trohpoh grahndeh/ trohpoh peekohloh/ trohpoh kahroh

known for its faïence ceramics, which take their inspiration from the Iberian pottery of Majorca in the 12th century. There you'll find striking plates, tiles and pots in a variety of designs in blue and yellow. The **International Museum of Ceramics** (🄴 Viale Baccarini 19 🅣 0546 697 311 🅦 www.micfaenza.org) details the history of the craft, and numerous factories and shops offer the ceramics for sale.

Eating & drinking

It's not for nothing that Bologna's nickname is *La Grassa* (The Fat): in a country obsessed with food, Bologna is undoubtedly the *grande dame*. While art historians marvel at Florence and fashionistas roam the streets of Milan, gastronomes flock here to dine in restaurants from the most expensive to the most humble, and to stock up on local produce from the markets and shops. And it is that local produce that has secured the Bolognese reputation. The whole region has long been an agricultural phenomenon, an ideal landscape for sheep rearing and pig farming, and a fertile region for growing fruit and wheat.

Italy has a bewildering number of words for its restaurants, but each one should indicate the kind of atmosphere and food to expect if you follow these basic guidelines: an *osteria* is a very simple, basic establishment, not dissimilar to a pub, serving rustic-style food. A *trattoria* is a step up from this, usually family run, and again serving simple dishes such as pasta. An *enoteca* (or, sometimes, *vineria*) is for wine only, although snacks such as olives and nuts may be served, while a *birreria* is predominantly a (beer-)drinking place, but will also serve simple dishes. A *ristorante* is the most formal option, usually complete with tablecloths and full menu. It's usually advisable to book ahead at a *ristorante*, particularly for an evening meal.

PRICE CATEGORIES

Prices are per person, for an average three-course meal, without drinks.

£ up to €35   ££ €35–50   £££ over €50

◉ *Enjoying an afternoon coffee in the sunshine*

Lunch is served between 12.00 and 15.00 and most places do not open in the evening until 20.00, with their kitchens closing at 23.00. The service charge (*il servizio*) is usually included in the bill (*il conto*); it may also be included as part of *il coperto*, the cover charge. The latter is usually around €1.50–3. In any case, it's always considered polite to leave a small tip.

Many an American child must have gone to school with a baloney sandwich in their lunch pack, but how many would actually have known that the name is derived from Bologna? In Italy this pork sausage, usually served in thin slices, is known as *mortadella*. Pork is integral to the Bolognese cuisine, unsurprisingly given the amount of pig farming in the region. Suckling pig has been a delicacy since the Middle Ages, and the salty cured ham from Parma is renowned the world over. *Zampon*, boned pigs' forelegs, stuffed with a mixture of ground pork, pork rinds and spices, are also a regular feature of local menus, although they may be an acquired taste. The other most famous product of the region is also from Parma. *Parmigiano Reggiano* (Parmesan), the hard, cow's-milk cheese, is a ubiquitous presence on the table of any Italian restaurant around the globe.

Most regions of Italy proudly claim their right to at least one, but usually more, pasta shapes, and Bologna is no exception. *Tortellini* – tiny pasta parcels filled with meat or cheese and served in soups or with a cream of tomato sauce – were purportedly inspired by Venus's navel, and so proud is the city of its creation that it even has a special name for a woman who makes them: a *sfoglina*. *Tagliatelle*, a wide, ribbon pasta usually served with meat and tomato sauce (*ragù*), also originates here, as does *pasta verde*, its pale green colour resulting from the inclusion of spinach in the

USEFUL DINING PHRASES

I would like a table for... people
Vorrei un tavolo per... persone
Vohray oon tahvohloh pehr... pehrsohneh

Excuse me!	**May I have the bill, please?**
Scusi!	Mi dà il conto, per favore?
Skoozee!	*Mee dah eel cohntoh pehr fahvohreh?*

Could I have it well cooked/medium/rare, please?
Potrei averlo ben cotto/mediamente cotto/al sangue, per favore?
Pohtray ahvehrloh behn kohtoh/mehdyahmehnteh kohtoh/ahl sahngweh, pehr fahvohreh?

I am a vegetarian. Does this contain meat?
Sono vegetariano/vegetariana (*fem.*). Contiene carne?
Sohnoh vehjehtehrehahnoh/vehjehtehrehahnah. Kontyehneh kahrneh?

pasta dough. *Pasta verde* is often used for another Bologna staple, the delicious layered pasta casserole dish, *lasagne*. And who hasn't reproduced their own version of spaghetti bolognese? In Bologna itself you'll see it listed as *spaghetti al ragù* (spaghetti in meat and tomato sauce).

As for wine, the region is not so well known for its wine production as its neighbour, Tuscany, but it does produce the soft, sweet and slightly sparkling Lambrusco.

Entertainment & nightlife

Italians are a gregarious lot who like to have fun, and Bologna is one of the most lively cities in terms of nightlife and entertainment. The fact that it is also a university town ensures that there's a vibrant mix of young and old, all adding to the atmosphere once the sun goes down. Be warned, however: Bologna is not a cheap city, so if you want to join in the fun you'll have to pay for it.

The evening starts to kick off at around 19.00, when the work day has ended and locals indulge in that most enduring of Italian traditions, the *passeggiata*. This is a time to stroll the streets, enjoy a cocktail or two in the innumerable bars (it is estimated that there are more than 200 *osterie* in Bologna, a tradition going back centuries) and catch up on gossip and news. The main centre for this activity is the pedestrianised Via Clavature, with its many outside tables jam-packed with revellers in the summer months. Once the initial socialising is over, people usually then head to a restaurant for dinner at around 21.00, lingering over the meal for at least a couple of hours. Dinner is an event in itself – Italians have no truck with an eat-and-run mentality. Then, finally, it's on to another bar for an after-dinner nightcap before heading home, unless you want to welcome in the early hours on a dance floor.

Again, the student fraternity means that there is no shortage of places for you to show off your moves in the city. The area around the university has plenty of nightlife offerings, although most of the more renowned and trendy nightclubs are in the northwest of the city and just outside. Most clubs charge an entrance fee of around €10–15, but you are entitled to at least one free drink in return. Clubbers must be over the age of 18, and you may be asked for some ID. Clubs go in and out of fashion and favour, so the best way to find

⬤ *Early-evening drinks in the piazza, before the nightlife kicks off*

◆ *Tower of the Palazzo Comunale by night*

out where the action is during your visit is to pick up *051* magazine, which is a free pamphlet found in bars and clubs.

Bologna is a relatively gay-friendly city. But Italy still has a macho culture, not to mention a religious one. While society is more tolerant now, open displays of gay affection will not be met with approval.

Bologna has long had a love affair with jazz, and many of the genre's great international names have performed here. Many of the *osterie* will have impromptu jam sessions.

The Bolognese love theatre, too, and there are plenty of venues around the city. Note, though, that almost all productions, even Shakespeare, are performed in Italian, so if you have limited knowledge of the language, you will simply have to enjoy the spectacle.

Like the rest of the world, cinema has taken over as the most popular cultural activity to enjoy on a regular basis. Italian cinema has long been a thriving industry and its output regularly wins international awards, but if you're hankering after a Hollywood blockbuster there are some cinemas in town that screen films in English.

There are free local multilingual newspapers, such as *CityBologna* and *Leggo Bologna*, available from the tourist office, which also have listings to find out what's going on. The **tourist board's website** Ⓦ www.bolognaturismo.info is updated frequently, and is in English as well as Italian.

Sport & relaxation

Football (*il calcio*) is the national passion in Italy and, as Bologna's team is in the premier league, *Serie A*, the city is addicted – in season matches are often screened in bars. But the city also offers plenty of other sporting options, both spectator and participatory.

SPECTATOR SPORTS

Basketball

Pallacanestro (as they call it) is the second most popular sport, and Bologna's two teams, Kinder Virtus and Fortitudo, are among the best in Europe. Buy tickets at the **Pala Malaguti** stadium (ⓐ Via Gino Cervi 2, Casalecchio di Reno ❶ 051 758 758) before the game.

Football

Football is played at the **Stadio Renato Dall'Ara** (ⓐ Via A Costa 174 ❶ 051 614 3844 ⓦ www.bolognafc.it), which was built in 1927 as one of Italy's first modern sports stadiums. Matches, however, usually sell out way in advance, so if you want to see the action you'll need to plan very well ahead.

PARTICIPATION SPORTS

Golf

There are several golf courses outside of Bologna, the best of which is the 18-hole **Golf Club Bologna** (ⓐ Via Sabattini 69, Chiesa Nuova di Monte San Pietro ❶ 051 969 100 ⓦ www.golfclubbologna.it), 8 km (5 miles) south of the city.

Skiing

The Apennines reach heights of 2,000 m (6,560 ft), and usually guarantee good snowfall in winter. There are over 20 ski resorts in the vicinity. Try Corno alle Scale/Budiara/Val Carlina (80 km/50 miles from Bologna, accessible by train from Porretta), Fiumalbo/Monte Cimone (take the train from Pistoia), or Sestola (67 km/40 miles from Modena, accessible by train from Porretta).

Swimming

Bologna has ten swimming pools, the most central of which are **Stadio** (ⓐ Via dello Sporto 174 ❶ 051 615 2520) and **Sterlino** (ⓐ Via Murri 113 ❶ 051 623 7034). Pool hours are generally 09.30–19.00, but it is worth phoning ahead to check.

Tennis

There are indoor and outdoor clay tennis courts at the **Centro Sportivo Record** (ⓐ Via Pilastro 8 ❶ 051 503 311).

RELAXATION
Hiking

Around Bologna are numerous beautiful national parks that contain hiking and biking trails and have bike-hire facilities. Contact the tourist office (see page 150) for information on the following parks: Parco dell'Alto Appennino Modenese, a great place to spot eagles; Parco del Delta del Po, with large areas of marshland, ideal for birdwatching; Parco del Sassi di Rocca Malatina, known for its peregrine falcons; and Parco dello Stirone, with its awesome canyons. Hiking trails are mapped out in red in the hills surrounding the city. Obtain maps from the tourist office or the **CAI** (Club Alpino Italiano ❶ 02 205 7231 ⓦ www.cai.it).

For avid walkers, the GEA (Grande Escursione Appenninica) is a 400-km (250-mile) trail that traces the Apennine mountain range from Liguria to Le Marche.

Accommodation

As a major commercial centre, Bologna has a good supply of hotel rooms. However, during the trade fair seasons of March to early May and September to December, as well as around Christmas, New Year, Easter and the Celebrazioni Madonna di San Luca (see page 10), accommodation is not only fairly scarce but also considerably more expensive than at other times of the year. Year-round, indeed, Bologna is not a cheap destination, and the range of budget options is far more restricted than in, say, Florence or Rome. Needless to say, the closer you are to the centre, the more you'll pay.

HOTELS & GUESTHOUSES
Albergo Pallone £ Not far from Piazza Maggiore, the Pallone is one of the best bets if you're on a shoestring budget. The rooms are clean but basic – they each have a washbasin, but baths and showers are communal. ❸ Via dell Pallone (The university quarter) ❶ 051 421 0533 ⓦ www.albergopallone.it ❷ info@albergopallone.it ❸ Bus: 20, 28, 36, 37, 89, 93, 94, 99

Panorama £ Centrally located, not far from Piazza Maggiore, this hotel offers a range of accommodation, from three- to four-bedded dormitory rooms to ordinary doubles, and shared bath facilities.

PRICE CATEGORIES
The ratings in this book are for a double room for one night (excluding VAT and breakfast).
£ up to €90   ££ €90–150   £££ over €150

🅐 Via Livraghi 1 (no sign), off Via Ugo Bassi (Piazza Maggiore & *centro storico*) ☎ 051 221 802 🅦 www.hotelpanoramabologna.it 🅝 Bus: 13, 14, 17, 18, 19, 20, 25, 28, 29, 30, 86, B, Aerobus BLQ

Marconi £–££ The Marconi offers no-frills basic, clean rooms, some with private baths. It is on a main road, however, so if traffic bothers you, ask for a room at the back. 🅐 Via Marconi 22 (Piazza Maggiore & *centro storico*) ☎ 051 262 832 🅦 www.pensionemarconi.it 🅝 Bus: 11, 13, 17, 18, 19, 21, 25, 28, 30, 36, 38, 39, 86, 89, 94, B, D, E

Rossini £–££ Comfortable, basic rooms, some with private baths. 🅐 Via dei Bibiena 11 (The university quarter) ☎ 051 237 716 🅦 www.albergorossini.com 🅝 Bus: 14, 19, 25, 27, C, B

Centrale ££ A former aristocrat's home, the Centrale is the best budget option. The rooms are spacious and those on the third floor have good views of the Due Torri (Two Towers) and the city. 🅐 Via della Zecca 2 (Piazza Maggiore & *centro storico*) ☎ 051 225 114 🅦 www.albergocentralebologna.it 🅝 Bus: 13, 14, 17, 18, 19, 20, 25, 28, 29, 30, 86, B, Aerobus BLQ

Garisenda ££ Rooms are on the third floor of a former *palazzo* so offer superb views of the Two Towers. Clean and friendly with free Wi-Fi. No lift. 🅐 Via Rizzoli 9, Galeria del Leone 1 (Piazza Maggiore & *centro storico*) ☎ 051 224 369 🅦 www.albergogarisenda.com 🅝 Bus: 13, 14, 19, 25, 27

Hotel Arcoveggio ££ A friendly and welcoming place to stay, only 15 minutes from the historic centre, with very modern rooms, all of which include free Wi-Fi connections. Breakfast is included, and there's the added advantage of on-site parking for a minimal charge. ⓐ Via Lionello Spada 27 (The university quarter) ⓣ 051 355 436 ⓦ www.arcoveggiohotel.com ⓥ Bus: 11, 27

Tuscolano ££ The Tuscolano offers the opportunity to sightsee all day then return to a genuine Italian community at night and eat in the local cafés and restaurants. All rooms have private bathrooms and there is on-site parking. Closed August. ⓐ Via del Tuscolano 29

● *A room at the elegant Hotel Arcoveggio*

(The university quarter) ☎ 051 324 024 🌐 www.hoteltuscolano.it
🚍 Bus: 27A

Beatrice Bed & Breakfast ££–£££ There are only three rooms here, but each is exquisitely decorated and you certainly get personal service – continental breakfast is served in your room. Shared bathroom. 🏠 Via dell'Indipendenza 56 (Piazza Maggiore & *centro storico*) ☎ 051 246 016 🌐 www.bb-beatrice.com 🚍 Bus: 20, 27, 28, A, Aerobus BLQ

Al Cappello Rosso ££–£££ Probably the most romantic and luxurious place to stay in Bologna, right by Piazza Maggiore. The building dates from 1375 and the red hat (*cappello rosso*) of its name refers to the headgear of the medieval tradesmen who stayed here. 🏠 Via de'Fusari 9 (Piazza Maggiore & *centro storico*) ☎ 051 261 891 🌐 www.alcappellorosso.it 🚍 Bus: 11, 17, 18, 20, 25, 27, 28, 29, 30, 86, A, B, BLQ

Art Hotel Orologio £££ A small, charming hotel that affords views of all the action in Piazza Maggiore. The rooms are elegant and comfortable and breakfast is included. 🏠 Via IV Novembre 10 (Piazza Maggiore & *centro storico*) ☎ 051 745 7411 🌐 www.bolognarthotels.it 🚍 Bus: 13, 14, 17, 18, 19, 20, 25, 28, 30, 38, 39, 86, A, B, Aerobus BLQ

Baglioni £££ You'll want for nothing here, from the free Wi-Fi and satellite TV in all the rooms, to the 24-hour concierge service, parking, personal shopper, shuttle service, tour guide and, for those who really want to show off, the option of your own personal butler. The hotel's restaurant is decorated with 16th-century frescoes, while the food itself is mouthwatering. 🏠 Via dell'Indipendenza 8 (Piazza Maggiore & *centro storico*) ☎ 051 225 445 🌐 www.baglionihotels.com 🚍 Bus: 11, 20, 27, 28, A, Aerobus BLQ

Hotel Cavour £££ One of Bologna's best-known and long-standing hotels in a very central location. ⓐ Via Goito 4 (Piazza Maggiore & *centro storico*) ⓣ 051 228 111 ⓝ Bus: 11, 20, 27, 28, A, C, Aerobus BLQ

Porta San Mamolo £££ A stylish and romantic option, just off Piazza Maggiore and close to the Due Torri. Some rooms have terraces overlooking the lovely garden, while those on the top floor benefit from a panorama of the entire city. Breakfast included. ⓐ Vicolo del Falcone 6–8 (Santo Stefano & around) ⓣ 051 583 056 ⓦ www.hotel-portasanmamolo.it ⓝ Bus: 29, 32, 33, 52

HOSTELS & CAMPSITES

It is compulsory to have either an AIG or AICS card for hostels in Bologna. AICS cards can be purchased directly at the hostels. You can purchase an AIG card from either the San Sisto Due Torri (see below) or the **National AIG Office** (ⓣ 064 871 152 ⓦ www.aighostels.com).

Centro Europa Uno £ There are eight bungalows, which can sleep up to six, a car park and a campsite, located 7 km (4½ miles) from the city centre. ⓐ Via Emilia 297 ⓣ 051 625 8352 ⓝ Bus: 101, 916, 918 ⓘ No credit cards

San Sisto Due Torri £ A modern (if bland) hostel 6 km (4 miles) from the city centre. Open 24 hours. ⓐ Via Viadagola 5 ⓣ 051 501 810 ⓦ www.ostellodibologna.com ⓝ Bus: 93 & 20 daytime, 21B evening & 301 Sundays ⓘ No credit cards

Centro Turistico Città di Bologna £–££ Located 4 km (2½ miles) outside the city, the site consists of bungalows, chalets (both of which have en-suite facilities) and pitches for tents, as well as a swimming pool, snack bar, playground and Internet centre. ⓐ Via Romita 12–4A ⓣ 051 325 016 ⓦ www.hotelcamping.com ⓝ Bus: 68

🔺 *The swimming pool at the Centro Turistico campsite*

THE BEST OF BOLOGNA

Whether you are on a flying visit to Bologna or taking a more leisurely break in Italy, the city offers sights and experiences – as well as tastes and sensations – that simply should not be missed.

TOP 10 ATTRACTIONS

- **Piazza Maggiore and La Fontana del Nettuno** The magnificent centrepiece of this grand city exerts a magnetic pull on visitors (see page 69).

- **Basilica di San Petronio** One of the largest churches in Christendom, it has a spectacular frescoed interior (see page 62).

- **Due Torri (Two Towers)** Torre degli Asinelli & Torre della Garisenda are two of the city's towers erected by powerful medieval families (see page 65).

- **Portico di San Luca** The finest portico in the city, with 666 arches and 15 chapels (see page 70).

- **San Giacomo Maggiore & l'Oratorio di Santa Cecilia** Beautiful frescoes in the former parish church of the Bentivoglio family (see page 72).

- **Palazzo Poggi and the university museums** A wealth of knowledge in a grand setting (see page 86).

- **Orto Botanico** One of the oldest botanical gardens in the world, established in the 16th century (see page 83).

- **Museo Ducati** Track the story of the famous motorbike (see page 48).

- **Museo Morandi** Houses the largest collection of works by Morandi, Bologna's best-loved modern artist (see page 73).

- **Museo Ebraico** Traces the turbulent history of Jews in Bologna (see page 85).

❯ *Palazzo del Podestà (see page 68) at night*

Suggested itineraries

HALF-DAY: BOLOGNA IN A HURRY

Soak up the lively atmosphere of Piazza Maggiore, admire the majestic Fontana del Nettuno (see page 69) then relish the quiet of the Gothic Basilica di San Petronio (see page 62) with its stunning altar, paintings and frescoes.

Difficult to miss are Bologna's best-known landmarks, Torre degli Asinelli and Torre della Garisenda, together known as the Due Torri (Two Towers, see page 65). In the 12th century Bologna had dozens of towers as status symbols – the more powerful the family that commissioned them, the taller they built the tower. All except these two were torn down in a 19th-century regeneration programme. The Torre degli Asinelli, built between 1109 and 1119, is 97 m (318 ft) high and has an inclination of 2.23 m (over 7 ft). The reward for walking up its 498 steps is a breathtaking panoramic view over city rooftops. The Torre della Garisenda was built in the same period as the Asinelli. It is shorter, at 48 m (157 ft) high, but its inclination is 3.22 m (over 10 ft). This tower is closed to the public.

1 DAY: TIME TO SEE A LITTLE MORE

Don't miss the church of San Giacomo Maggiore (see page 72), which was the parish church of the wealthy Bentivoglio family, and is now renowned for its 15th-century frescoes in the chapel. The Oratorio di Santa Cecilia is also noteworthy for its frescoes illustrating the life of the saint. While admiring all the porticoes in the city, don't fail to pop over to look at the Portico di San Luca (see page 70), stretching 4 km (2½ miles) up the Colle della Guardia and including 666 arches and 15 chapels.

2–3 DAYS: TIME TO SEE MUCH MORE

A few more days give you time to enjoy some of the city's many museums, such as the Museo Ducati (see page 48) and its factory, where the famous motorcycles – the equivalent of a Ferrari on two wheels – are made and exhibited. Also worth visiting are the Museo Morandi (see page 73), with over 200 works by Giorgio Morandi, Bologna's most famous contemporary artist; the Museo Ebraico (see page 85), which explores Jewish history in the region over the course of the last 4,000 years; or the recently opened Biblioteca Salaborsa, built on top of Etruscan remains (see page 65).

Bologna has a total of 21 university museums, but you're unlikely to have either the time or inclination for all of them. However, the the University's Orto Botanico (Botanical Gardens, see page 83), one of the oldest in the world, has over 100,000 dried plants on display, and flora fans should make time for a visit. The grounds are ablaze with hundreds of varieties of Mediterranean flora.

LONGER: ENJOYING THE AREA TO THE FULL

With a little longer to explore, you'll have time to follow the Portico di San Luca right up into the hills to visit the Santuario della Madonna di San Luca (see page 70), which is connected to the city walls by the world's longest portico, an impressive 4 km (2½ miles) long. As well as finding room for this on your camera, you'll also want to immortalise the panoramic views from here of the city down below. Extra time in the region will allow you to get in touch with your inner gastronome: Bologna is also an excellent starting point for trips to Parma (see page 106), famous for its cheese and ham. Also well worth a visit is Ferrara (see page 130), with its *palazzi* and cultural attractions, and Ravenna (see page 120), with its extraordinary Byzantine mosaics.

Something for nothing

While no one could argue that Bologna is a cheap destination, the great advantage of its historic centre is that its streets are made for walking. Simply strolling through the piazzas and porticoes offers enough delights to occupy a whole morning, or even a whole day, while spending very little. No visitor will want to miss the magnificent Piazza Maggiore, the adjoining Piazza Nettuno and the fabulous Fontana del Nettuno (see page 69). The great Bolognese churches, in particular Basilica di San Petronio (see page 62) and San Giacomo Maggiore (see page 72), with their wonderful artworks, offer a peaceful respite from the streets outside. The cathedral, too, is worth a visit: the Cattedrale di San Pietro (see page 65) houses an *Annunciation* by Ludovico Carracci (1555–1619), founder of the Bolognese School of painting.

Housed within a 16th-century *palazzo*, the free **Museo delle Cere Anatomiche 'Luigi Cattaneo'** ('Luigi Cattaneo' Wax Museum ⓐ Via Irnerio 48 ① 051 209 1556 ⓦ www.museocereanatomiche.it) might seem like a rather macabre place to visit, but it would be a shame to leave Bologna without seeing the waxworks. Models of various parts of the human body, all hand-sculpted, were used until the 19th century for medical demonstrations and instruction, and are so artistically skilled and accurate that they have a strangely appealing quality.

One of the nicest walks in the city is from Via Saragozza to Via San Luca on the Monte della Guardia, where the Santuario della Madonna di San Luca (see page 70) is located, at the end of the Portico di San Luca. Not only is it an opportunity to visit this revered pilgrimage site, but the views from here are spectacular and are free to enjoy. The walk takes time and is strenuous in places but well worth the effort.

Bologna is a sophisticated city, where designer names abound: it doesn't cost anything to window-shop and to dream. Among the trendsetters are Furla on Via D'Azeglio, Prada and Salvatore Ferragamo on Via Farini, MaxMara and Stefanel on Via Rizzoli, and Gucci, Versace and Emporio Armani in Galleria Cavour.

🔺 *You can stroll all day through the city's medieval streets*

When it rains

The northern Italian climate, while mild, is not immune to a little rainfall every now and then, particularly if you are visiting in low season. But this need not put an end to your enjoyment of the city – many of Bologna's unmissable treasures are found in museums, churches, and even underground.

La Casa Carducci (House of Carducci ⓐ Piazza Carducci 5 ⓘ 051 347 592 ⓦ www.casacarducci.it) was a former 16th-century church. It was deconsecrated in 1798, and in 1890 became home to the great Tuscan poet Giosuè Carducci (1835–1907), whose works were a rallying cry for the unification of Italy. Following his death, one of his most ardent fans, Queen Margherita of Savoy, bought the house in order to preserve the writer's artefacts and possessions, and it has operated as a museum since the 1920s. Among the items on display are Carducci's original desk and writing equipment, as well as a vast library. Since 1990 this has also been the home of the Museo Civico del Risorgimento, exploring the run-up to and the final unification of the Italian states in 1860 (see page 17).

Museo Ducati (ⓐ Via Ducati 3 ⓘ 051 641 3343 ⓦ www.ducati.com), in the grounds of the company that first produced the legendary Ducati motorcycle in 1946, displays bikes through the decades. It also presents the motorbikes' success in racing championships and iconic images of some of their more famous riders.

A rainy day will give you the ideal chance to see a totally different and hidden aspect of the city's history. Among the highlights of an underground tour are the **Bagni di Mario** (Mario's Baths), the elaborately decorated 16th-century cistern that, among other things, supplied water for the Fontana del Nettuno, and the Torrente Aposa (Aposa Torrent), a 1st-century BC network of tunnels that are the source of historic trivia. Access to the baths is by tour guide only and booking is essential. Contact a **Bologna tour guide** (① 051 467 598 ⓦ www.bolognatourguide.com) or the **Associazione amici delle vie d'acqua e dei sotterranei di Bologna** (① 051 623 2255 ⓦ www.amicidelleacque.org), which promotes awareness of the role of water in the city's history.

🔺 *Take shelter in one of Bologna's many beautiful churches*

On arrival

TIME DIFFERENCE

Italy is on Central European Time (CET). During Daylight Saving Time (late Mar–late Oct) clocks are set ahead one hour.

ARRIVING

By air

Marconi International Airport (☏ 051 647 9615 ⒲ www.bologna-airport.it) is the main airport serving Bologna and is located 6 km (4 miles) northwest of the city centre. All arrivals come into Terminal A. On departure all European and domestic services leave from Terminal A while intercontinental flights leave from Terminal B. The airport has money-changing facilities, a bank, restaurant and shops. The tourist information desk, serviced by English-speaking staff, is located in the centre of the arrivals terminal.

Aerobus (☏ 051 290 290 ⒲ www.atc.bo.it), the city's airport link, has a shuttle service that runs in a loop stopping at both terminals, then at the following stops in the city centre: Ospedale Maggiore, Via Ugo Bassi, Via dell'Indipendenza/San Pietro, Via dell'Indipendenza/Arena del Sole and the FS Stazione Centrale. Buses run every 15 minutes between 07.30 and 20.00, and tickets (around €5 one way) can be purchased on board. It's the most cost-efficient way of getting to and from the airport and the city, but traffic can be appalling, particularly during rush hour, so the journey can take about an hour. There is also a *servizio diretto* (direct link) that runs from the airport to the Fiera district during trade shows.

Forlì Airport (☏ 0543 474 990 ⒲ www.forliairport.com), located 60 km (40 miles) from Bologna, is the airport of choice for the low-cost airlines, but access is not easy. To get to Bologna city centre,

⬥ *An aerial view with the Palazzo Comunale in the foreground*

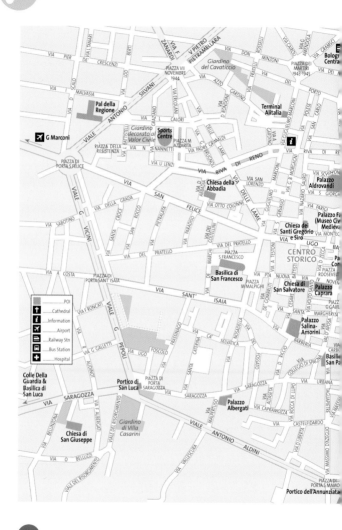

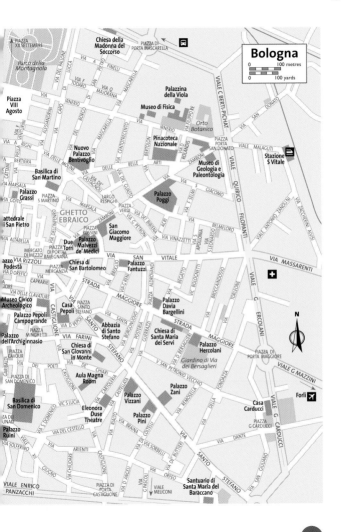

Bologna

| 0 | 100 metres |
| 0 | 100 yards |

the easiest option is to take the direct bus service to the bus station on Piazza XX Settembre. Buses are not particularly frequent, running every one to two hours. Journey time is approximately one hour and thirty minutes, and tickets cost about €10. Be sure to check the schedule carefully if you plan to return to the airport using this bus service. Alternatively, hop on the €3.50 Aerobus to Forlì's main train station, where connections to and from Bologna are frequent.

By rail

Bologna is a major hub for the FS (Ferrovie dello Stato) rail network, with frequent fast connections to Venice, Florence, Milan, Ravenna, Rimini and almost anywhere else in Italy. The Stazione Centrale (Central Station) is on the north side of the city centre, about a 15-minute walk up Via dell'Indipendenza to Piazza Maggiore. If you're carrying heavy luggage, however, and don't want to walk, bus numbers 10, 25 or 30 also take you into the centre – purchase a ticket from *tabaccherie* (tobacconists), newsstands or ticket machines. The Italian State Railway, Trenitalia, is one of the most economical in Europe, with fares in both directions charged by the kilometre.

🛈 Note that no ticket is valid until it has been stamped, before boarding, in one of the yellow machines on the platform. You might face on-board fines if the ticket is unvalidated.

Stazione Centrale 🅰 Piazza Medaglie d'Oro 🕿 051 258 3059
Trenitalia 🕿 892 021 from within Italy only 🔘 www.trenitalia.com

By road

National Express (🔘 www.nationalexpress.com) operates a service from London Victoria to Bologna for the most budget-restricted traveller. The trip takes more than 24 hours, including stops in Paris and Milan.

IF YOU GET LOST, TRY ...

Excuse me, do you speak English?
Mi scusi, parla inglese?
Mee skoozee, pahrlah eenglehzeh?

Excuse me, is this the right way to the old town/the city centre/the tourist office/the station/the bus station?
Mi scusi, questa è la strada giusta per la città vecchia/
il centro/l'ufficio informazioni turistiche/la stazione ferroviaria/
la stazione degli autobus?
*Mee skoozee, kwestah eh lah strahdah justah pehr la cheetah
vehkyah/eel chentroh/loofeecho eenfohrmahtsyonee
tooreesteekah/lah statsyoneh fehrohveeahreeyah/
lah stahtsyoneh dehlyee owtohboos?*

With low-cost airlines now serving the city, this is only an option for those who positively prefer travelling by road. Bologna's main bus station, the **Autostazione** (☎ 051 245 400 ⓦ www.autostazionebo.it), is near the mainline station at Piazza XX Settembre.

For those intending to visit by car, the *autostrada* approaching Bologna skirts around the city to the north in a ring road, the *tangenziale*, which connects to the major routes. Bologna is linked by the A1 to Milan (two hours), Florence (one hour) and Rome (three hours), by the A13 to Venice and Padua, and by the A14 to Rimini, Ravenna and the Adriatic coast. All motorways in Italy charge tolls, so if you want to avoid these costs (approximately €15 from Rome to Bologna, for example) opt for the *strade statali* (state roads) or SS, which are toll free. Within the *tangenziale* the state roads leading into

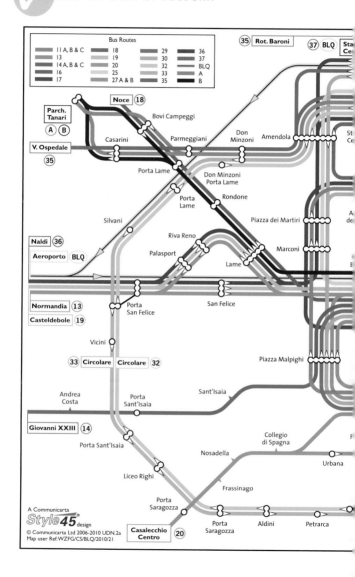

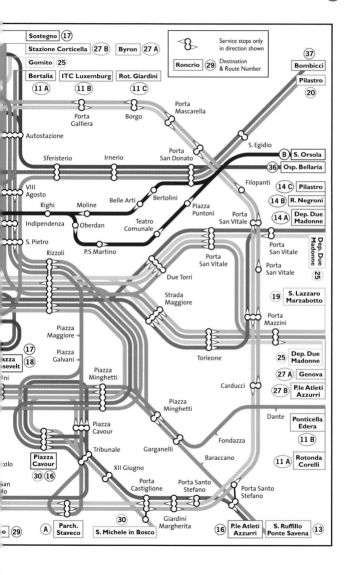

Bologna connect up to an inner ring road around the city centre.
Since the centre is closed to traffic, you will be routed around it on
the ring of boulevards that follows the course of the demolished
city walls. There are 16 clearly marked car parks around the edge of
the city centre. Each of these is connected to the downtown area by
frequent bus services.

FINDING YOUR FEET
It can't be said too many times: the best way to see Bologna is
on foot. This way you can marvel at the ingenuity that went into
the building of the 60 km (40 miles) of porticoes, the churches,
the university and the *palazzi*. Early in the morning is the optimal
time of day for immersing yourself in Bologna's centuries of history.
In the evening, after a day spent walking, garner an outside seat at
a local *osteria* and absorb the vibrant nightlife around you. This is
the most enjoyable and effective way of educating yourself about
the people whose city you are visiting.

ORIENTATION
The heart of Bologna is its Roman core, Piazza Maggiore, at the
junction of the city's two main roads, Via Ugo Bassi and Via Rizzoli.
These roads are the new face of the old Via Emilia, the famous
Roman road that at one time traversed the entire region. The
area now called the *centro storico* (historic centre) is ringed by
the *circonvallazione*, the busy perimeter road that follows the
demarcation of the old city walls, joining up at the 12 city gates.

GETTING AROUND
Take advantage of the city's efficient local bus system, the
ATC (☎ 051 290 290 ⓦ www.atc.bo.it). Before boarding any bus

you must purchase a ticket. These are available from tobacconists, newsagents, which you will find strewn around the city, or the tourist office (see page 151). Tickets are valid for one hour and can be used on as many buses as you want, but, as with trains, you must validate them by using the punching machine when you get on board. They cost about €1. If you plan to make frequent use of the bus service, purchase a CityPass, which costs around €8.50 and is valid for ten journeys.

At Marconi International the taxi rank is outside Terminal A. The journey usually costs €15–20, depending on traffic, which is usually heavy. The price can be higher if you have a substantial amount of luggage. Alternatively, you can call a taxi on ✆ 0513 72727.

CAR HIRE

Unless it's absolutely necessary, you should avoid driving in Bologna – cars are restricted in the city centre, and for the most part parking is non-existent. In addition, the local driving style is on the crazed side of enthusiastic and could induce collapse before familiarity is achieved. If you must drive, the following companies have offices at at least one of the airports and in Bologna proper, mostly along the northern end of Via Marconi/Via Amendola. If you're planning to tour around the region, it's usually more economical to book a fly/drive package from your home country.

Before leaving the car park, make sure you have all necessary documentation and that you know how to operate the vehicle. Remember to drive on the right-hand side of the road.

Autoeuropa ⓦ www.autoeuropa.it
Marconi airport ✆ 051 647 2006

Avis Ⓦ www.avisautonoleggio.it
Forlì airport ❶ 0543 781835
Marconi airport ❶ 051 647 2032
ⓐ Via Marco Polo 91 ❶ 051 634 1632

EasyCar Ⓦ www.easycaritalia.com
Forlì airport ❶ 0543 473436

Europcar Ⓦ www.europcar.it
Forlì airport ❶ 0543 473241
Marconi airport ❶ 051 647 2111
Bologna ⓐ Via Boldrini 22/B ❶ 051 353 665

Hertz Ⓦ www.hertz.it
Marconi airport ❶ 051 647 2015
Bologna ⓐ Via Amendola 16 ❶ 051 254 830

Sixt Budget Ⓦ www.sixt.it
Forlì airport ❶ 0543 782 981
Marconi airport ❶ 051 647 2052
Bologna ⓐ Via Pietramellare 35 ❶ 051 241 442

▶ *The Baroque Santuario della Madonna di San Luca*

THE CITY OF
Bologna

Piazza Maggiore & the *centro storico*

The *centro storico* (historic centre) and the surrounding pedestrianised streets should be any visitor's first port of call. Piazza Maggiore, once the site of the Roman forum and, until the 19th century, still the main trading area of the city, remains to this day a bustling cultural centre. At any given time of day you may come across a group of schoolchildren kicking a football about, students lounging over their books, or business people stopping for a quick gossip on their way to another meeting. The geographical heart of the city is also its social core.

SIGHTS & ATTRACTIONS

Basilica di San Domenico
The highlight of this 13th-century church is, unsurprisingly, the ornate tomb of San Domenico, crafted by great artists of the day, including Nicola Pisano, Guglielmo, Nicola dell'Arca, Alfonso Lombardi and even a young Michelangelo. The latter's *San Procolo* figure decorating the tomb shows clear indications of the artistry that would eventually lead to the creation of *David* and many other masterpieces. ⓐ Piazza San Domenico 13 ⓣ 051 640 0411 ⓛ 09.30–12.30, 15.30–18.30 Mon–Fri, 09.30–12.30, 15.30–17.30 Sat & Sun ⓥ Bus: 16, 30, 38, 39, 52, 58, 59, A, B, E

Basilica di San Petronio
The most important church in Bologna, the Basilica di San Petronio is also one of the largest in Christendom. Although it looms over the Piazza Maggiore, the 14th-century façade is sadly unremarkable – rumour has it that when the Vatican heard that there were plans to make it grander than St Peter's in Rome, they carefully reallocated funds elsewhere and the exterior was never finished.

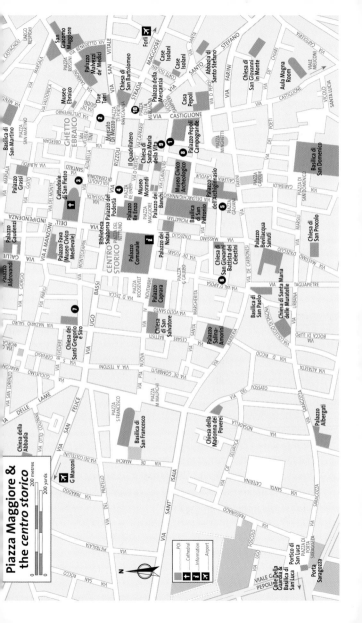

Piazza Maggiore & the centro storico

200 metres
200 yards

POI
Cathedral
Information
Airport

N

Chiesa della Abbadia

G Marconi

Palazzo Aldrovandi

Palazzo Gaudenzi

Basilica di San Martino

San Giacomo Maggiore

Palazzo Malvezzi de' Medici

Museo Ebraico

GHETTO EBRAICO

Due Torri

Chiesa di San Bartolomeo

Case Isolani

Case Isolani

Abbazia di Santo Stefano

Chiesa di San Giovanni in Monte

Aula Magna Room

Palazzo della Mercanzia

Casa Pepoli

Mercato di Mezzo

Il Quadrilatero

Chiesa di Santa Maria della Vita

Palazzo Pepoli Campogrande

Palazzo Grassi

Cattedrale di San Pietro

Museo Morandi

Palazzo Re Enzo

Palazzo del Podestà

Palazzo dei Banchi

Museo Civico Archeologico

Basilica di San Domenico

Biblioteca Salaborsa

CENTRO STORICO

Palazzo Comunale

Basilica di San Petronio

Palazzo dei Notai

Basilica di San Giovanni in Monte

Palazzo Fava (Museo Civico Medievale)

Palazzo Caprara

Chiesa di San Salvatore

Chiesa di San Giovanni Battista dei Celestini

Palazzo Salina-Amorini

Palazzo Bevilacqua Samuti

Chiesa di San Procolo

Chiesa dei Santi Gregorio e Siro

Basilica di San Francesco

Basilica di Santa Maria delle Muratelle

Basilica di San Paolo

Chiesa di Santa Maria delle Muratelle

Chiesa della Madonna dei Poveri

Palazzo Albergati

Colle della Guardia & Basilica di San Luca

Portico di San Luca

Porta Saragozza

The interior, however, certainly doesn't disappoint. Among the highlights are the *Madonna and Child* and carvings and bas-reliefs depicting stories of the Old Testament by Jacopo della Quercia, frescoes detailing the life of San Petronio, Bologna's patron saint, and the spectacular *Martyrdom of Saint Sebastian* on the altar by Lorenzo Costa.

In total there are 22 chapels in the basilica, with paintings, sculptures, glasswork and faïence by many Bolognese artists, but the most compelling is the Cappella Bolognini (Bolognini Chapel), financed by the Bolognini family's silk empire, with frescoes by Giovanni da Modena entitled *The Journey of the Kings*, *Paradise* and *Hell*. ⓐ Piazza Maggiore ❶ 051 231 415 ⓛ daily 09.30–12.30, 15.00–18.00 (Nov–Mar); 09.30–12.30, 15.30–18.00 (Apr–Oct) Ⓝ Bus: 11, 13, 14, 17, 18, 19, 20, 25, 27, 29, 30, 86, A, B, Aerobus BLQ ❶ No bags

○ *Take shelter from the sun in the cloisters of the Basilica di San Domenico*

other than ladies' handbags allowed inside; there is nowhere to deposit any other kind of bag, so don't take one.

Biblioteca Salaborsa

The recently opened library is a wonderful resource open to the public and provides reading rooms, study spaces and computers, Wi-Fi access, free newspapers and a café. The Etruscan remains can be glimpsed through the glass floors and the main library itself is worth a visit. ⓐ Piazza Nettuno 3 ❶ 051 219 4400 ⓦ www.bibliotecasalaborsa.it ❶ 14.30–18.00 Mon, 10.00–20.00 Tues–Fri, 10.00–19.00 Sat, closed Sun

Cattedrale di San Pietro

It's easy to lose sight of Bologna's cathedral, dwarfed as it is by more recent and more impressive buildings at the heart of the busy Via dell'Indipendenza. But look out for the 13th-century marble lions that grace the entrance and you'll have found your spot.

Inside, too, the building is a bit of a hotchpotch of styles from over the centuries, each one added to repair or replace damage caused by fires or earthquakes. Highlights, however, include Ludovico Carracci's *Annunciation* in the sacristy.

The main event in the cathedral each year is during the Festa di San Luca in May, when the icon of the saint is brought here from her hillside shrine, the Santuario della Madonna di San Luca. ⓐ Via dell'Indipendenza 9 ❶ 051 222 112 ❶ 08.00–12.00, 16.00–18.15 daily ⓝ Bus: 11, 27, A, Aerobus BLQ

Due Torri (Two Towers)

These two leaning towers may stand out as beacons today, but in the Middle Ages, when they were built, they were just two of more than 100 such landmarks, built to illustrate the importance and wealth of each noble family that ordered their construction. Others do still exist around the city, but none is as majestic. It's possible to climb the tallest tower, the Torre degli Asinelli, at 96 m (320 ft); if you have a head for heights, this offers some of the finest views over the rooftops of the historic centre. The smaller Torre della Garisenda, at 48 m (157 ft), however, is closed to the public. ❸ Piazza di Porta Ravegnana ⏱ daily 09.00–18.00 (Apr–Oct); 09.00–17.00 (Nov–Mar) Ⓝ Bus: 11, 13, 14, 19, 20, 25, 27, 29, 30, A, B ❶ Admission charge

Palazzo dei Banchi

The Palazzo dei Banchi (Bankers' House), on the eastern side of Piazza Maggiore, is the area in which money-lenders traditionally set up their benches (*banchi*) to do business. The building is most notable for its classical façade, designed by the architect Vignola in the 16th century, and for its elegant arcades, which are still referred to as Il Pavaglione, because the cocoons of the *pava* (silkworm) were sold here during the Middle Ages. ❸ Piazza Maggiore ⏱ Closed to the public Ⓝ Bus: 1, 3, 13, 14, 17, 18, 19, 20, 25

Palazzo Comunale (Town Hall)

The Palazzo Comunale, aka Palazzo D'Accursio, today combines various architectural styles from the 13th to the 15th centuries, as various city dignitaries added to the building. The original structure dates from 1287, but further additions were made in 1365 and again in 1425. The most notable feature of the façade is the statue of Pope Gregory XIII, peering down over the main entrance. Inside, the first floor of the *palazzo* holds a museum, the Collezioni Comunali d'Arte, which is home to various important works of art, most notably in the Sala di Ercole (Hercules' Room) featuring a statue of the eponymous

◆ *The Asinelli and Garisenda towers*

god by Alfonso Lombardi. Among other works here are Ludovico Carracci's *Phaeton's Fall* and the *Madonna and the Earthquake* by Francesco Francia. Paintings and frescoes also adorn the Sala Farnese, with works by the Carracci brothers and Tintoretto, among others.
ⓐ Piazza Maggiore ⓣ 051 203 629 ⓛ 09.00–15.00 Tues–Fri, 10.00–18.30 Sat & Sun, closed Mon ⓝ Bus: 11, 13, 14, 17, 18, 19, 20, 25, 27, 29, 30, 86, A, B, BLQ Aerobus ⓘ Admission charge during special exhibitions (phone to check)

Palazzo dei Notai

Tucked neatly between the Basilica di San Petronio and Palazzo Comunale is the modest, Gothic-style Palazzo dei Notai (House of the Notaries), originally dating from the 13th century. For centuries this was home to the Guild of Notaries, where Bologna's residents would come to seek legal advice and representation. ⓐ Via Pignattari 1 ⓛ For special exhibitions only (phone to check) ⓝ Bus: 11, 13, 14, 19, 20, 25, 27, 29, 30, A, B

Palazzo del Podestà & Palazzo Re Enzo

The corner of Piazza Maggiore and Piazza del Nettuno is occupied by these two *palazzi*, originally dating from the 13th century but much altered over the years. The Palazzo del Podestà, the city's main law court, was entirely renovated in 1484 under the instruction of the influential Giovanni II Bentivoglio, and today only the Arengo Tower, built in 1212, remains of the original structure. The pillars surrounding the tower are decorated with terracotta statues representing the city's eight patron saints, masterfully sculpted by Alfonso Lombardi.

The Palazzo Re Enzo is named after Enzo, illegitimate son of Emperor Frederick II, the 13th-century king of Sicily and Holy Roman Emperor. During one of the continued skirmishes between the papal loyalists (Guelphs) and the supporters of the empire (Ghibellines), the Guelphs defeated Frederick in 1249 and took Enzo as their prisoner. He was incarcerated in this building for 22 years, until his death in 1271, although by all accounts his imprisonment was not too arduous: he led a sybaritic life enhanced by poetry and women, and was tended to by servants. ❸ Piazza del Nettuno, Piazza Re Enzo ❺ Both *palazzi* are closed to the public except during exhibitions Ⓝ Bus: 11, 13, 14, 19, 20, 25, 27, 29, 30, A, B

Piazza Maggiore

The hub of public life in Bologna, Piazza Maggiore exerts an almost magnetic pull on visitors and locals, and inevitably you will start or end up here. The piazza's antechamber, Piazza Nettuno, is graced by the exquisite Fontana del Nettuno (Fountain of Neptune), designed in 1563 by Tommaso Laureti and embellished with the work of Flemish sculptor Jean de Boulogne (known in Italian as Giambologna). Around

⬣ *Piazza Maggiore*

⬤ *Portico di San Luca, the longest arcade in the world*

Il Gigante, as Neptune is affectionately known, Giambologna also sculpted many *putti* (cherubs) and mermaids. Very near here, on Palazzo Comunale, is another fountain, referred to as La Fontana Vecchia (Old Fountain), which was also designed by Tommaso Laureti and is indeed older than the Fountain of Neptune. ⓝ Bus: 11, 13, 14, 19, 20, 25, 27, 29, 30, A, B

Portico di San Luca

At the Porta Saragozza begins the portico to beat all porticoes. Traversing 4 km (2½ miles), all the way up the Colle della Guardia to the Santuario della Madonna di San Luca, and taking in some 666 arches and 15 chapels en route, it has the impressive honour of being the longest continuous arcade in the world. This extraordinary feat of architectural engineering was created by Giovanni Monti, begun in 1674 and completed in 1739. ⓝ Bus: 20

LA FAMIGLIA BENTIVOGLIO – WARRIORS AND PATRONS

The Bentivoglio family was one of the great warring dynasties of medieval Bologna. Not only did they wield immense political power over the region at a time when Italy was divided into many different states and kingdoms, but they were also visionaries in that they saw the advancement and procurement of art as a signature of wealth and prestige. At the height of their power in 1460, Sante Bentivoglio sought to set their importance in stone with the building of a large family *palazzo* on Via Zamboni. But it was Sante's son, Giovanni II, who contributed most to the city in terms of art and architecture. During his 46-year reign, Bologna became a hotbed of artistic activity, most notably with the school of Francesco Francia, also known as Francesco Raibolini (1450–1517), and in the buildings around the university quarter, which was the family's stronghold. The city's fortunes always mirrored those of the family; times were changing, however – by 1506 Bologna had become a papal state and Giovanni II was overthrown and exiled. But perhaps through nostalgia or romanticism, the family is still remembered in various parts of the city.

Il Quadrilatero and Il Mercato di Mezzo

To the east of Piazza Maggiore is an area known as Il Quadrilatero (roughly 'the rectangle'), a labyrinthine area of medieval alleyways. From Roman times onwards this was the heart of the trading area of the city, and many of the streets are named after the merchants that once plied their wares here: *orefici* (jewellers), *clavature* (locksmiths), *pescherie* (fishmongers), *drapperie* (textile merchants) and more.

The spirit of commerce still fills the air with the daily Mercato di Mezzo, stalls piled high with fresh fruit and vegetables, as the traders call out to customers and passers-by advertising their produce. At night, however, a more genteel atmosphere pervades as the lights from the fashionable bars and cafés shine down on their chic clientele. Bus: 13, 14, 19, 25, 27

San Giacomo Maggiore & l'Oratorio di Santa Cecilia

It goes at least some way to explaining the vast wealth of the noble families of Bologna in the Middle Ages when you consider that the spectacular San Giacomo Maggiore was the parish church of the Bentivoglio family. It was Giovanni Bentivoglio II who commissioned the artist Lorenzo Costa to complete three frescoes in the Bentivoglio Chapel – the *Triumph of Death*, the *Apocalypse* and a *Madonna Enthroned* – surrounding in self-indulgent manner the family tombs. Costa also worked, alongside Francesco Francia and Amico Aspertini, at Giovanni's request, on scenes illustrating the life of Saint Cecilia in the oratory dedicated to the saint. Piazza Rossini, Via Zamboni 15 051 225 970 07.00–12.00, 15.00–18.30 daily Bus: 14, 19, 25, 27, C

CULTURE

Museo Civico Archeologico (Archaeological Museum)

Formerly a hospital for the terminally ill, this impressive 14th-century building is now home to an equally impressive collection of archaeological relics. Perhaps not surprisingly, since they were the first civilisation in the region, the highlight of the collection is the Etruscan section, with displays of jewellery, coins and other finds. The Egyptian section, too, is superb, including an eerie gathering of mummies in the basement. Greek and Roman sculpture (copies, not originals) and a section on

prehistoric finds complete the experience. ⓐ Via dell'Archiginnasio 2
ⓣ 051 275 7211 ⓒ 09.00–15.00 Tues–Fri, 10.00–18.30 Sat & Sun,
closed Mon ⓝ Bus: 11, 13, 14, A, B ⓘ Admission charge for special
exhibitions only

Museo Morandi

Giorgio Morandi (1890–1964) is Bologna's best-loved modern artist
and this museum is entirely dedicated to his work, with more than
300 paintings on display. Also in the museum is a reconstruction
of his study, including his easel, brushes and other tools of his
trade. ⓐ Palazzo D'Accursio, Piazza Maggiore 6 ⓣ 051 203 332

△ *Museo Civico Archeologico*

Ⓦ www.museomorandi.it Ⓛ 09.00–15.00 Tues–Fri, 10.00–18.30 Sat & Sun, closed Mon Ⓝ Bus: 11, 13, 14, 17, 18, 19, 20, 25, 27, 29, 30, 86, A, B, Aerobus BLQ

RETAIL THERAPY

Bologna is a shopper's paradise – whatever you are looking for. Food, clothes, antiques and books are among the best buys; every Italian designer has a flagship store here, and the innumerable delicatessens, as well as open-air markets, offer a mouthwatering array of Bolognese specialities. The presence of the university also ensures a wide range of bookshops.

L'Inde le Palais This classy 'concept store' sells a little bit of everything – clothing, accessories, furnishings, perfumes, CDs and even books in English. The shop even has its own café across the way for you to rest your feet and admire your purchases. Ⓐ Via de' Musei 6 Ⓣ 051 648 6587 Ⓛ 15.30–19.30 Mon, 10.30–14.00 & 15.30–19.30 Tues–Fri, 10.30–19.30 Sat, closed Sun Ⓝ Bus: 20, 29, 30

Majani Chocoholics beware – enter Majani and you may end up buying their entire stock! This delectable *cioccolataio* has been in this spot since 1796 and produces the famous 'Fiat' range. Ⓐ Via De'Carbonesi 5 Ⓣ 051 234 302 Ⓦ www.majani.com Ⓛ 09.00–13.00, 15.30–19.30 Mon–Sat, closed Sun Ⓝ Bus: 20, 38, 94, D

Mercato delle Erbe This vast covered market oozes with the sights and aromas of stall upon stall of fresh fruit and vegetables. Ⓐ Via Ugo Bassi 2 Ⓛ 07.15–13.15 Mon–Sat, 17.00–19.30 Mon–Wed & Fri, closed Sun Ⓝ Bus: 3, 14, 17, 18, 19, 20, 25, 28, 29, 30, 86, B, Aerobus BLQ

Paris Texas Italy This is the place to come if you want designer gear from the likes of Dolce & Gabbana and Versace at bargain prices.
🔵 Via Altabella 11 ☎ 051 225 741 🕐 09.30–13.00, 15.00–19.00 daily
🚍 Bus: 14, 17, 18, 19, 25, 28, 86, B

Tamburini Probably the best food shop in the city – choose from an incredible array of home-made pastas, local hams and cheeses.
🔵 Via Caprarie 1 ☎ 051 234 726 🕐 08.00–19.00 Mon–Sat, closed Sun
🚍 Bus: 1, 3, 13, 14, 17, 18, 19, 20, 25

TAKING A BREAK

Bistro 18 £ ❶ If your feet are weary from pounding the porticoes, stop off at Bistro 18 for a cappuccino or one of the delicious first courses. 🔵 Via Clavature 18 ☎ 051 273 014 🕐 7.00–24.00, closed Tues

Due Torri £ ❷ A very central, good-value lunch option, with the added benefit of a range of vegetarian choices. 🔵 Via De' Giudei 6
☎ 051 237 718 🕐 Dinner only: 18.00–23.00 Mon–Sat, closed Sun
🚍 Bus: 11, 20, 29, 30 ❗ No credit cards

Faccioli £ ❸ A great place to stop for a drink, in the shadow of one of the city's towers. 🔵 Via Altabella 15B ☎ 051 223 171 🕐 18.00–23.00
Mon–Sat, closed Sun 🚍 Bus: 1, 3, 13, 14, 17, 18, 19, 20, 25

La Torinese £ ❹ Anyone with a sweet tooth should make a beeline here – the hot chocolate is quite simply delicious, as are the pastries. 🔵 Piazza Re Enzo 1A ☎ 051 236 743 🕐 07.00–20.00 daily
🚍 Bus: 11, 20, 29, 30, A

Zanarini ££ ❺ This elegant and highly traditional café with its uniformed staff is the perfect place to enjoy a coffee and a sweet pastry. ⓐ Piazza Galvani ⓣ 051 275 0041 ⓝ Bus: 11, 13, 20, 96

AFTER DARK

RESTAURANTS

Le Navate Café £–££ ❻ Tucked away on a tiny street near Via Barberia, this friendly *trattoria* is simple in style but superb in quality and service. ⓐ Via Val D'Aposa 7E ⓣ 051 262 793 ⓛ 12.00–14.30, 17.30–20.30 Tues–Sat, closed Sun & Mon ⓝ Bus: 30, 39, A

Montegrappa del Nello ££ ❼ The house specialities here include *tortellina Montegrappa* (*tortellini* served in cream and meat sauce), *graminia* (thin spaghetti served with truffles, mushrooms and cream) and wonderful salads of mushrooms, truffles, Parmesan cheese and artichokes. ⓐ Via Montegrappa 2 ⓣ 051 236 331 ⓛ 12.00–15.00, 19.00–23.30 Tues–Sun, closed Mon ⓝ Bus: 20, 28, A ⓘ Reservations are recommended

Taverna Del Postiglione ££ ❽ For some wonderful traditional cuisine at good-value prices, you couldn't do better than to stop in at this warm and charming restaurant. The handmade *tortelloni* are particularly recommended. ⓐ Via Marchesana 6 ⓣ 051 263 052

Trattoria Gianni ££ ❾ One of the most traditional dishes on the menu here is *bolliti*, a local meat stew, or choose a pasta dish. The wine list, too, concentrates on the local region. ⓐ Via delle Clavature 18 ⓣ 051 229 434 ⓛ 12.30–14.30, 19.30–22.30 Tues–Sat, closed Sun & Mon ⓝ Bus: 11, 20, 29, 30

Ristorante Pappagallo (The Parrot) £££ ❿ Don't miss the opportunity to dine in Bologna's best restaurant, sitting in the shadows of the Due Torri within a 14th-century *palazzo*. The *lasagna verdi al forno* (baked lasagne with spinach) is a house speciality and try one of their delicious desserts. ⓐ Piazza della Mercanzia 3C ❶ 051 232 807 Ⓦ www.alpappagallo.it ⓛ 12.30–14.30, 19.30–22.30 Mon–Sat; closed Sun & three wks in Aug Ⓝ Bus: 1, 3, 13, 14, 17, 18, 19, 20, 25 ❶ Reservations recommended

CINEMAS

The following cinemas screen some films in English:

Adriano English films each Monday. ⓐ Via San Felice 52 ❶ 051 555 127 Ⓝ Bus: 13, 19, 36, 38, 81, 87, 91, 92, 93

Cinema Chaplin English films each Wednesday. ⓐ Piazza di Porta Saragozza 5 ❶ 051 585 253 Ⓝ Bus: 20, 33, 39, 94, D

Nosadella Films in their original language. ⓐ Via Nosadella 19/21 ❶ 051 331 506 Ⓦ www.nosadella.it Ⓝ Bus: 14, 20, 21, 38, 89, 94, E

CLUBS & BARS

Cassero Bologna's most famous gay club. ⓐ Via Don Minzoni 18 ❶ 051 649 4416 ⓛ 21.30–24.00 Sun & Mon, 19.00–24.00 Tues & Thur (Thur is ArciLesbica night), 21.30–02.00 Wed, 21.30–03.00 Fri, 21.30–05.00 Sat Ⓝ Bus: 33, 35, A

Chet Baker You can dine and listen to live jazz here. ⓐ Via Polese 7 ❶ 051 223 795 Ⓦ www.chetbaker.it ⓛ 21.00–late Wed–Sat, closed Sun–Tues

The university quarter

As home to the oldest university in Europe, it's not surprising that Bologna is often referred to as *Bologna la Dotta* (Bologna the Learned). The university began life in 1088 as a unique institution – it was the students themselves who set it up and organised its management, including the hiring of lecturers and professors. Its first speciality was the study of law, which laid the foundations for modern legal practice, followed by philosophy and medicine; it became known particularly as a centre for the study of anatomy and astronomy. It was an alumnus of Bologna, Vacarius, who set up the law department of that other great seat of learning, Oxford University, in 1144. Today the university is still the most respected in Italy. The main area of the university quarter is Via Zamboni, where lively cafés buzz with the chatter of philosophising students. However, the area is known for more than just learning: the city's theatre district is by Piazza Verdi, there's elegant shopping to be done along Via Oberdan and antique shops can be found on Via San Vitale, while the Ghetto Ebraico (Jewish ghetto) remains an atmospheric area of narrow alleyways and cobbled lanes.

SIGHTS & ATTRACTIONS

Chiesa di San Bartolomeo

This tiny 16th-century church, dwarfed by the Due Torri (see page 65), is rather unprepossessing outside, but its real gem is its interior frescoes, including *San Carlo al sepolcro di Varallo* by Ludovico Carracci, one of Bologna's finest Renaissance artists. ⓐ Piazza di Porta Ravegnana ⓣ 051 227 692 ⓛ 07.00–13.00, 16.00–19.00 daily ⓝ Bus: 14, 19, 25, 27

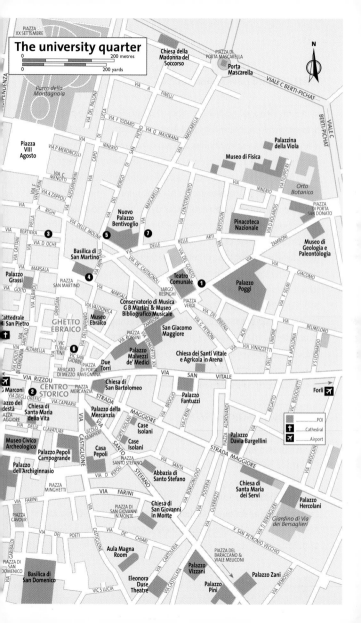

Ghetto Ebraico (Jewish Ghetto)

Although Bologna's Jewish community was not only tolerated but also respected in the Middle Ages, the anti-Jewish measures laid down by the papal bull (charter) of 1555 condemned Jews to live in a segregated area, known as a ghetto, and restrict their trades to money-lending and medicine. The Jews remained in these confined conditions, behind elegant Via Rizzoli, until the middle of the 19th century: names of some streets such as Via dell'Inferno (Street of Hell) clearly illustrate how they felt about their life and situation. Some buildings still sport spyholes in the doors, which indicates the suspicion and fear of persecution that afflicted the Jews' everyday lives. Despite its unhappy past, however, today the area is an atmospheric enclave of narrow alleyways and old buildings, many of which now house excellent restaurants. To learn more about the city's Jewish heritage, visit the Museo Ebraico (see page 85).

Another place in the area that belies its past is the Galleria Acquaderni, an elegant shopping centre that still sports ancient frescoes on some of its walls. In its past life, the building was a church, the Chiesa di San Giobbe, then a much-feared hospital for those suffering from *mal francese* ('French evil' or syphilis).

The area is also home to many of the medieval towers constructed by wealthy families at the time: the Torre degli Uguzzoni in Vicolo Tubertini, the 11th-century Torre Prendiparti in Via Sant'Alo, Casa-torre Guidozagni near Via Albiroli, and the Torre degli Azzoguidi on Via Caduti di Cefalonia. ⓐ Ghetto Ebraico Ⓝ Bus: 11, 13, 14, 19, C

Nuovo Palazzo Bentivoglio

The Bentivoglio family was the most powerful in Bologna in the Middle Ages, but by the end of the 15th century the tide had turned, and in 1507 their grand palace was pulled down by less subservient

⬧ *Wander the alleyways of the Ghetto Ebraico*

🔺 *One of the few canals left in Bologna*

VIA DELLE MOLINE AND BOLOGNA'S CANALS

One of Bologna's early disadvantages was that it had no natural water source, so in the 12th century a canal system was put in place that dammed water from the River Reno to divert into the city. This not only provided much-needed drinking water and sanitation, as well as powering the silk and hemp mills that were at the centre of Bologna's trade in the Middle Ages, but it also allowed goods and materials to be imported and exported north to the River Po. By the early 20th century, however, industrialisation and the advent of motor traffic meant that the canals had become redundant, and they were paved over. Some are just visible, though: at the bridges on Via Piella, Via Capo di Lucca and Via Alessandrini you can still see water flowing beneath the streets.

citizens. Perhaps through guilt, or perhaps through realising there was a value in history, this new *palazzo* was then built a few years later in their honour. Today it is home to private residences and offices, but visitors can take a look at the courtyard with its lovely Romanesque *loggias*. ❷ Via delle Belle Arti 8 Ⓝ Bus: 20, 28, 36, 37, C

Orto Botanico (Botanical Gardens)

Bologna's Orto Botanico was first established in 1568, making it one of the oldest such institutions in Europe; its popularity has never waned. The plants were initially intended to assist medical students at the nearby university, and to explore the healing qualities of different species. Today there are ornamental gardens, greenhouses filled with exotic plants from around the world, a woodland park and a man-made pond breeding lilies and other wetland plants. Without question, spring is the best time to visit, when the plants are a riot of colour. ❸ Via Irnerio 42 ❶ 051 209 1299 ⏰ 08.00–15.00 Mon–Fri, 08.00–13.00 Sat, closed Sun Ⓝ Bus: 20, 28, 36, 37, 89, 93, 94, 99

Piazza VIII Agosto

Unless you're a real history buff, there's nothing in the early part of the week to draw you to this square (which takes its name from the date the Bolognese defeated the Austrians in the First War of Italian Independence in 1848). But later in the week it becomes a bustling, colourful marketplace (see page 24) that attracts anyone and everyone in Bologna who's in search of bargain books, leather goods, china and a whole host of other paraphernalia. A sister market is held up the steps in Parco della Montagnola. Ⓝ Bus: 11, 20, 27, 28, 36, 37, 89, 93, 94, 99, A, C

Teatro Comunale

Built on the site of the former Bentivoglio Palace by Antonio Bibiena in 1763, this theatre has been entertaining the Bolognese for more than three centuries (see page 91). Although the present façade only dates from 1933, when Mussolini altered the frontage of so many buildings, the auditorium boasts a wonderful tier of Baroque boxes on either side of the stage. ❸ Largo Respighi 1 ❶ 051 529 958 (info line call centre, where you will find opening hours' details) Ⓦ www.tcbo.it Ⓝ Bus: 14, 19, 25, 27, C

Via San Vitale

This is the place to come if you're in search of antiques, or simply want to escape the lively student atmosphere of Via Zamboni. But it's also worth visiting for the *palazzi* behind the long portico, some of which are open to the public. Palazzo Orsi at No 28 is known for its Baroque statues, the façade of Palazzo Fantuzzi at No 23 is decorated with incongruous elephant motifs, while the Palazzo Scagliarini-Rossi at No 56 was the 19th-century home of Cornelia Rossi, a legendary society hostess in her day.

Bus: 14, 19, 25, 27, C

CULTURE

Conservatorio di Musica G B Martini & Museo Bibliografico Musicale

When Napoleon briefly conquered Italy at the turn of the 19th century, he deconsecrated many buildings, including this former Augustinian convent. Instead, it became Bologna's music conservatory, which can count many great musicians and composers among its alumni, including Verdi, Rossini and Puccini. The highlight of the conservatory is the concert hall, with a huge organ at its heart and the walls decorated with portraits of composers down the centuries. There is also a musical museum on site, containing many priceless works such as autographed scripts and scores, the original score of Rossini's 1816 opera *The Barber of Seville*, historical instruments and portraits of composers, including one of Johann Christian Bach by Thomas Gainsborough. Piazza Rossini 2 051 221 117 www.conservatorio-bologna.com 09.00–13.00 Mon–Fri; closed Sat, Sun & Aug Bus: 14, 19, 25, 27, C

Museo Ebraico (Jewish Museum)

When Bologna became a papal state in the 16th century, the Jewish community, who had previously lived and worked alongside the rest of the population, was forced to move to a gated ghetto on the east side of the historic centre. Nevertheless, Jews continued to make an important contribution to city life, particularly in trade. This relatively new museum, in the heart of the former ghetto, examines the history of Jews in the city through the ages, including the tragedy of World War II. It also hosts regular lectures and workshops on the theme of Jewish identity, and other related topics. ⓐ Via Valdonica 1/5 ⓣ 051 235 430 ⓦ www.museoebraicobo.it ⓛ 10.00–18.00 Sun–Thur, 10.00–16.00 Fri; closed Sat & during Jewish holidays ⓝ Bus: 14, 19, 20, 25, 27, C ⓘ Admission charge

Palazzo Poggi and the university museums

Bologna's original university was housed in the Archiginnasio, just off Piazza Maggiore, but in 1803, under the instructions of Napoleon, its faculties were all united under one roof in the Palazzo Poggi, previously home to the Poggi family and then a science laboratory. It remains the main building of the university to this day. The grand interior is decorated with numerous murals, including *Ulysses* by Tibaldi, *The Labours of Hercules* by Nicolo dell'Abate and biblical scenes by Propero Fantana, all dating from the early 16th century. The *palazzo* is best known today, however, as home to many of the university museums. The Museo Navale has an impressive collection of nautical maps and model warships, the Museo di Architettura Militare explores the history of military architecture, including models of Baroque fortifications, and the Museo di Astronomia contains many instruments used in the 18th and 19th centuries to study the stars, as well as a fresco of the constellations and exhibits detailing the history of astronomy. ⓐ Via Zamboni 31–33 ⓣ 051 209 9602 ⓦ www.museopalazzopoggi.unibo.it ⓛ 10.00–13.00 Tues–Sun,

◆ *A quiet corner of Europe's oldest university*

closed Mon (mid-June–July & first 2 wks of Sept); 10.00–13.00, 14.00–16.00 Tues–Fri, 10.30–13.30, 14.30–17.30 Sat & Sun, closed Mon (mid-Sept–mid-June); closed Aug Bus: 14, 19, 20, 25, 27, 28, 36, 37, C

Pinacoteca Nazionale (National Gallery)

Almost no Italian city is without its art treasures, and Bologna's Pinacoteca Nazionale is a must for art lovers and historians alike. Among the collections are works by Tibaldi, Reni, the Carracci brothers and Guercino, painters from Bologna's most productive period, the early 17th century. The highlight, however, must be Raphael's *Ecstasy of Saint Cecilia* (c. 1515). Via delle Belle Arti 56 051 420 9411/421 1984 www.pinacotecabologna.it 09.00–19.00 Tues–Sun, closed Mon Bus: 20, 28, 36, 37, 89, 93, 94, 99 Admission charge

RETAIL THERAPY

Given that this is the university quarter, it's not surprising that the area is famous for its bookshops. Obviously most stock will be in Italian, but larger stores such as Libreria Feltrinelli (see below) will sell foreign-language books.

Libreria Feltrinelli The main branch of Italy's best bookstore chain. Piazza di Porta Ravegnana 051 266 891 www.lafeltrinelli.it 09.30–18.00 Mon–Sat, closed Sun Bus: 11, 17, 28, A, C

Libreria delle Moline Large selection of new and old books. Favoured by students and bookworms. Via delle Moline 3 051 232 053 10.00–12.30, 15.30–19.30 Mon–Wed, Fri & Sat, 10.00–12.30 Thur, closed Sun Bus: 20, 28, 36, 37, C

TAKING A BREAK

Del Teatro £ ❶ An attractive place for a drink, opposite the Teatro Comunale, hence its name. ⓐ Via Zamboni 26 ① 051 224 147 ⓛ 08.00–20.30 daily ⓝ Bus: 21, 38

Eataly Bologna £ ❷ This lively café, situated in a food and wine market and bookshop, is a perfect place to snack, eat or just enjoy a coffee. ⓐ Via degli Orefici 19 ① 051 095 2820 ⓦ www.eataly.it ⓛ 08.00–24.00 Mon–Sat, 10.00–24.00 Sun

AFTER DARK

RESTAURANTS
La Mariposa £ ❸ One of the most authentic *trattorie* in the city and a perennial favourite with the locals. Not only is the food fresh and delicious but it's good value, too. ⓐ Via Bertiera 12 ① 051 225 656 ⓛ 12.00–15.00 Mon–Sat; 19.00–23.00 Tues, Wed, Fri & Sat, closed Sun ⓝ Bus: 11, 20, 27, 28, A, C

Osteria dell'Orsa £ ❹ Famous for its *ragù alla Bolognese*, this place is a favourite hangout for students. ⓐ Via Mentana 1 ① 051 231 576 ⓛ 12.00–23.30 daily ⓝ Bus: C

La Stanze £ ❺ Set in the private chapel of the Nuovo Palazzo Bentivoglio, built in 1576, you can gaze at the 16th-century frescoes while tucking in to a simple but good plate of pasta. ⓐ Via del Borgo di San Pietro 1 ① 051 228 767 ⓛ 11.00–01.30 Mon–Fri, 18.00–24.00 Sat; closed Sun, July & Aug ⓝ Bus: 20, 28, 36, 37, 89, 93, 94, 99

Benso ££ ❻ Tucked into a side street in the old Jewish ghetto, this family-owned restaurant serves traditional Bolognese cuisine. It is particularly known for its desserts, such as *gelato ripieno all frutta* (fruit-filled ice cream). There is also a courtyard for dining alfresco.

🔺 *Teatro Comunale's beautiful interior*

Ⓐ Vicolo San Giobbe 3 Ⓣ 051 223 904 Ⓛ 12.00–01.00 Mon–Sat, closed Sun Ⓑ Bus: 14, 19, 25, 27

Bravo ££ ❼ A good-value trattoria that is particularly renowned for its live music. In July and August you can dine outside. Ⓐ Via Mascarella 1 Ⓣ 051 266 1122 Ⓦ www.bravocaffe.it Ⓛ 19.00–03.00 daily Ⓑ Bus: C

BARS, CLUBS & GIGS

Cantina Bentivoglio A wonderful kitchen, some great wine and live music swings here in a friendly atmosphere. For the full programme check their website. Ⓐ Via Mascarella 4 Ⓣ 051 265 416 Ⓦ www.cantinabentivoglio.it Ⓛ 20.00–02.00 daily

La Scuderia Bar, restaurant, music and dance venue, La Scuderia is always busy. Ⓐ Piazza Verdi 2 Ⓣ 051 656 9619 Ⓦ www.lascuderia.bo.it Ⓛ 08.00–02.00 daily

THEATRES

Arena del Sol Ⓐ Via dell'Indipendenza 44 Ⓣ 051 291 0910 Ⓦ www.arenadelsole.it Ⓑ Bus: 11, 20, 27, 28, A, Aerobus BLQ

Teatro Comunale The city's traditional classical music venue, in existence since the 18th century. Also the venue for the acclaimed opera season from November to June. Tickets are available from the box office, but for the opera you'll need to book well in advance. Ⓐ Largo Respighi 1 Ⓣ 051 529 958 (info line call centre) Ⓦ www.tcbo.it Ⓑ Bus: 14, 19, 25, 27, C

Teatro Dehon Ⓐ Via Libia 59 Ⓣ 051 342 934 or 344 772 Ⓦ www.teatrodehon.it Ⓑ Bus: 37, 60

Santo Stefano & around

Traditionally, the eastern side of Bologna has always been the smartest district and it was in this part of the city that all the noble families made their home in the Middle Ages. The main piazzas and streets – Via Santo Stefano, Via Castiglione, Piazza Santo Stefano and Strada Maggiore – each have a distinct character and, given the wealth of the area over the centuries, are naturally lined with grand *palazzi* and landscaped gardens as well as important churches. Strada Maggiore was also once part of the Roman Via Emilia, the important trade route that linked Piacenza and the Adriatic coast.

SIGHTS & ATTRACTIONS

Abbazia di Santo Stefano

Probably one of the most important areas of worship in Bologna and a spectacular example of Romanesque architecture, there were originally seven churches here in total, built in the eighth century over a pagan temple. Today, however, only four churches remain, dating from the 11th century. The Chiesa di Crocifisso (Church of the Crucifix) is notable for its simplicity; it has only a nave and a crypt, but it also leads to the Chiesa di San Sepolcro, which contains the tomb of San Petronio, one of the patron saints of Bologna. So important was the saint to the city that it was deemed entirely fitting to offer him such an elaborate burial site, reportedly modelled on the Holy Sepulchre in Jerusalem. The courtyard of this church is known as Piazza di Pilatus (Courtyard of Pontius Pilate) because in ancient times the 8th-century basin of its fountain was thought to be the one used by Pontius

● *Romanesque architecture of Abbazia di Santo Stefano*

Pilate to wash his hands after he had condemned Christ to death. The Romanesque cloisters of this church complex feature a series of plaques commemorating citizens of Bologna who have given their lives in times of war. Outside, the cobblestones of the triangular Piazza Santo Stefano are one of the most photogenic areas of the city. ➋ Via Santo Stefano 24 ❶ 051 223 256 ❿ www.abbaziasantostefano.it ❶ 09.00–12.00, 15.30–18.00 daily ❿ Bus: 11, 13, 19, 25, 27, 29, 30, 90, 96, C

Basilica di Santa Maria dei Servi

The first things to strike you about this Gothic 14th-century church are the frescoes by Vitale da Bologna, considered by many to be the 'father' of Bolognese painting. His work features in abundance in the interior, too, but the most priceless artwork is the *Madonna and Child* by Cimabue. The convent and sacristy also house 17th- and 18th-century paintings by artists from the acclaimed Bologna School. ➋ Strada Maggiore 43 ❶ 051 226 807 ❶ 08.00–12.00, 16.00–20.00 daily ❿ Bus: 14, 19, 25, 27

Casa Isolani & Corte Isolani

Via Santo Stefano and the Strada Maggiore are linked by a pretty passageway, the Corte Isolani, via a string of courtyards, dating from the 12th to the 16th centuries and today filled with restaurants, boutiques and cafés. At the end of the passageway are two houses, La Casa Isolani, which belonged to rich merchants during the Middle Ages who made their livings selling Grecian wares. The house on Piazza Santo Stefano features a spiral staircase by Vignola, while the one on Strada Maggiore has an impressive 10 m (30 ft) high portico. ➋ Via Santo Stefano & Strada Maggiore ❿ Bus: 11, 13, 14, 19, 25, 27, 90, 96, C

Chiesa di San Giovanni in Monte

Although the body of this church was built in the 13th century, the façade that greets visitors today is 15th century, constructed in Venetian style. The interior, however, is pure Gothic, and enhanced by artworks from the likes of Francesco del Cossa and Guercino, and by the *Crowning of the Virgin* altarpiece by Lorenzo Costa. Above the wooden door is a terracotta statue of an eagle, the symbol of St John, by Niccolò dell'Arca. ⓐ Piazza di San Giovanni in Monte ⓣ 051 263 894 ⓛ 07.30–12.00, 16.00–19.00 daily ⓝ Bus: 11, 13, 19, 90, 96, C

Conservatorio & Santuario di Santa Maria del Baraccano

After walking through an elegant 15th-century portico you reach the Santuario di Santa Maria del Baraccano, commissioned by Giovanni Bentivoglio II (see page 71) who added so much to Bologna's landscape. Above the church is the Conservatorio del Baraccano, established in 1531 as a school for poor girls. ⓐ Piazza del Barracano 2 ⓣ 051 392 680 ⓛ 11.00–13.00, 17.30–19.30 Sat, 10.00–12.30 Sun, closed Mon–Fri ⓝ Bus: 11, 19

Palazzo Bolognini

A short walk up Via Santo Stefano from the *loggia* brings you to what was the house of another of Bologna's powerful families, the Bologninis, who represented the feudal agriculture of the nobility and whose chapel is a feature of the San Petronio church (see page 62). Dating from the 16th century, the house has the nickname Palazzo delle Teste (Palace of the Heads), because of the many busts that look down on to the street. They are attributed to the sculptor Alfonso Lombardi (1487–c. 1536). ⓐ Via Santo Stefano 9/11 ⓝ Bus: 14, 19, 25, 27

Palazzo della Mercanzia

Since being built by Antonio di Vincenzo and Lorenzo da Bagnomarino in 1384, this has been the seat of the Chamber of Commerce, Industry, Agriculture and Crafts for Bologna. Constructed of brick and Istrian stone, the main features of the façade are its Gothic arches. The stunning columns and balcony are by the father-and-son team of Giovanni and Pietro di Giacomo.

ⓐ Piazza della Mercanzia, Via Santo Stefano ⓣ 051 609 3111 ⓛ Varies (phone ahead) Ⓝ Bus: 11, 13, 14, 19, 20, 25, 27, 29, 30, A, B

Strada Maggiore

This has been one of Bologna's most important streets since ancient times, forming part of the Roman Via Emilia (see page 92): within the shop at No 11 you can see a small piece of the original road that has been excavated and preserved. Today the street is lined with a series of former noble residences. At No 44 the most striking features of the Palazzo Davia Bargellini façade are its two statues of Atlas on both sides of the entrance, supporting the balcony above. The building is now home to the **Museo Davia Bargellini** (ⓣ 051 236 708), which displays the art collection of this noble family. Spanning the 14th to the 18th centuries, the collection includes a *Madonna and Child* by Cristoforo da Bologna and *La Pietà* by Simone dei Crocefissi. In the same building is the **Museo Civico d'Arte Industriale** (ⓣ 051 236 708), which has a fine collection of textiles, glassware and furniture from various eras.

Via Santo Stefano

Via Santo Stefano is most notable for its impressive mansions that were once home to some of the city's wealthiest families. Also here,

PIAZZA SAN DOMENICO

The main feature of this quiet square is the Basilica di San Domenico, whose highlight is undoubtedly the arca, or canopy, to the tomb of the saint, designed by the 13th-century sculptor Nicola Pisano with contributions from other Bolognese artists. The canopy was sculpted by Niccolo de Bari but it was so admired that he was forever after referred to as Niccolò dell'Arca. He died before all the statuettes were done, leaving the figures of San Petronius and San Procolus to be completed by his student, Michelangelo. Michelangelo also carved the kneeling angel on the front of the tomb. In the centre of the square is a column topped with a statue of the Virgin Mary that gives thanks for the end of a plague in 1632. Ⓝ Bus: 16, 30, 38, 39, 52, 58, 59, A, B, E

at No 31, is the Teatro dal Corso, which is most famous for having witnessed the debut of Gioacchino Rossini in 1811 with his opera *L'Equivoco Stravagante*. The Palazzo Finzi-Contini at No 33 was once a hotel, whose past guests have included the novelist Giorgio Bassani and one of Italy's greatest poets, Giacomo Leopardi.
Ⓝ Bus: 14, 19, 25, 27

RETAIL THERAPY

Bang Bang 2 You won't find any bargains here, but you will find collections from several designers under one roof, including Moschino, Versace and Sonia Rykiel. ⓐ Piazza Mercanzia 5 ⓣ 051 263 814 ⓛ 09.00–13.30, 15.30–19.30 Mon–Wed, Fri & Sat, 15.30–19.30 Thur, closed Sun Ⓝ Bus: 14, 19, 25, 27

⬥ *Piazza San Domenico*

Branchini Calzoleria Another place to splash your cash (this is the smartest area of the city, after all) on exquisitely cut dresses and hand-stitched shoes. ⓐ Strada Maggiore 19 ⓣ 051 648 6642 ⓦ www.branchini.net ⓛ 09.30–13.00, 15.30–19.00 Mon–Sat (Sat opening 10.00), closed Sun ⓝ Bus: 14, 19, 25, 27

Mercato Antiquario One of the best antiques markets in the city – come early if you want to secure some good bargains. ⓐ Via Santo Stefano ⓛ Sat & Sun every second wk ⓝ Bus: 11, 13, 20, 29, 30, C

TAKING A BREAK

Bricco d'Oro £ ❶ Morning or afternoon, this is a great spot for a cup of hot chocolate topped with peaks of whipped cream. It's a short walk from Piazza Maggiore, and in the early evening it makes an ideal pre-dinner pit stop for an aperitif. ❷ Via Farini 6 ❶ 051 236 231 🕐 07.30–20.30 daily 🚌 Bus: 11, 13, 19, 29, 38, 30, 52, E

Casa Godot Wine Bar £ ❷ This neighbourhood bar has a remarkable wine list with more than 1,000 to choose from, so whatever your grape preferences you should find something you like here. The menu is limited but good, offering selections of mortadella and assorted cheeses. ❷ Via Cartoleria 12 ❶ 051 226 315 🕐 08.00–01.00 Mon–Sat, closed Sun 🚌 Bus: 11, 13, 14, 19

Sorbetteria Castiglione £ ❸ Some locals will cross the entire city for the ice creams here. Try out more unusual concoctions such as mascarpone with caramelised pine nuts and white chocolate and hazelnut crunch. Next door is an equally delectable sweet shop – a chocolate version of the Due Torri is a great souvenir to take home. ❷ Via Castiglione 44 ❶ 051 233 257 🖥 www.lasorbetteria.it 🕐 08.00–24.00 Mon–Sat, 08.00–23.00 Sun 🚌 Bus: C

Mokarabia Cafè ££ ❹ More expensive than most cafés, but the cappuccinos are delicious and the surroundings are elegant. ❷ Strada Maggiore 23/C ❶ 051 849 1593 🕐 08.00–22.00 Mon–Sat, closed Sun 🚌 Bus: 14, 19, 25, 27

AFTER DARK

RESTAURANTS
Ristorante Grassilli £ ❺ A tiny spot that's well worth picking. It specialises in traditional Bolognese dishes, including home-made pasta. Walls are decked out with black-and-white photos of celebrities who have dined here. ❷ Via del Luzzo 3 ❶ 051 222 961

🕐 12.30–14.30, 19.30–22.30 Mon, Tues & Thur–Sat; closed Wed, Sun & two weeks in Aug 🚌 Bus: 11, 13, 14, 19, 20, 25, 27, 29, 30, A, B

Clorofilla £–££ ❻ A rare thing in Italy, but this is an organic vegetarian restaurant with a menu that goes to great lengths to explain the health benefits of all the ingredients. Even if you're a committed carnivore, it's a great place for delicious salads. Some non-veggie options available. ⓐ Strada Maggiore 64 ☎ 051 235 343 🕐 12.00–15.00, 19.30–24.00 Mon–Sat, closed Sun 🚌 Bus: 14, 19, 25, 27, C

Degli Angeli £–££ ❼ The name means 'tavern of the angels' and the dishes here are certainly close to heavenly. Simple food, lovingly prepared. ⓐ Via Farini 31 ☎ 051 268 032 🕐 12.00–24.00 Mon–Sat, closed Sun 🚌 Bus: 11, 13, 90, 96, A

Antica Osteria Romagnola ££ ❽ Housed in a 17th-century building, the Romagnola offers a wonderful array of pastas, as well as another local speciality, *capretto* (roast goat). ⓐ Via Rialto 13 ☎ 051 263 699 🕐 19.30–23.00 Tues, 12.30–14.30, 19.30–23.00 Wed–Sun, closed Mon 🚌 Bus: 11, 13, 19 ❶ Reservations recommended for dinner

Da Ercole ££ ❾ Typical Bolognese cuisine, with an emphasis on fish dishes and large salads. Popular with older locals. Located on a leafy piazza, there is seating outside in season. ⓐ Piazza Minghetti 2 ☎ 051 228 848 🌐 www.ristorantedaercole.com 🕐 12.30–15.30, 19.30–23.00 Wed–Mon; closed Tues & two weeks in Aug 🚌 Bus: 11, 13, 19, 20, 29, 30, 90, 96

Leonida ££ ❿ A relaxed, welcoming atmosphere greets diners at this friendly restaurant, where the house specialities are asparagus

⬥ *A backstreet in Bologna*

lasagne and tagliatelle with peas. ⓐ Vicolo Alemagna 2
ⓣ 051 239 742 ⓛ 12.30–15.00, 19.30–24.00 Mon–Sat, closed Sun
ⓝ Bus: 14, 19, 25, 27, C

Le Mura ££ ⓫ Its out-of-the-way location means that this is
more of a locals' haunt, but it's worth the effort to come here
and sample the delicious menu at good-value prices. ⓐ Vicolo
Falcone 13 ⓣ 051 644 9717 ⓛ 12.30–14.30, 19.30–24.00 Tues–Sun,
closed Mon ⓝ Bus: 29, 52

Trebbi ££ ⓬ You don't stay in business for 50 years if the
customers don't like what they're served. Trebbi has been
pleasing local palates with its traditional cuisine for more than
half a century. ⓐ Via Solferino 40 ⓣ 051 583 713 ⓛ 11.00–14.00,
18.00–23.00 Mon–Fri, 18.30–24.00 Sat, closed Sun ⓝ Bus: 15, 16, 29,
30, 39, 59, A, E

Drogheria della Rosa £££ ⓭ A cosy restaurant that used to be
a food store, hence the name *drogheria* (which means 'grocer's')
and the original doors and furnishings. The food is superb, and
there's an exceptional wine list. ⓐ Via Cartoleria 10 ⓣ 051 222 529
ⓦ www.drogheriadellarosa.it ⓛ 12.30–15.00, 20.00–23.00 Mon–Sat,
closed Sun ⓝ Bus: C

Dè Poeti £££ ⓮ One of the oldest *osterie* in Bologna, the setting
of Dè Poeti in the 14th-century Palazzo Senatorio is almost as good
as its food. For a more lively evening, get a table in the large dining
room, where there is live music three times a week. ⓐ Via dei Poeti 1
ⓣ 051 236 166 ⓦ www.osteriadepoeti.com ⓛ 12.30–14.30 Tues–Fri,
19.30–01.00 Tues–Sun, closed Mon ⓝ Bus: 11, 13, 16, 30, 38, A

BARS, CLUBS & DISCOS

Chalet Giardini Margherita Built in 1888 for the Emiliana Regionale Exhibition, this chalet is located on a small island in the Giardini Margherita gardens. These days, it's one of the best spots for dancing till dawn. ⓐ Viale Meliconi 1 ⓣ 051 307 593 ⓦ www.chaletdeigiardinimargherita.it ⓛ 23.00–03.00 Sun–Thur, 23.00–04.00 Fri & Sat Ⓝ Bus: 11, 17, 21, 25, 38, 30, 36, 38, 61, 62, 81, 87, 89, 91, 92, 93, 94, 97, 98, D

Kasamatta A very trendy three-floor disco-pub. ⓐ Via Sanpier 3 ⓣ 051 224 256 ⓛ From 21.00; dancing from 01.00 Tues, Fri & Sat

MUSIC & THEATRE

Good venues for music and theatre are:

Accademia Filarmonica ⓐ Via Guerrazzi 13 ⓣ 051 222 997 ⓦ www.accademiafilarmonica.it

Basilica di Santa Maria dei Servi This lovely church (see page 95) stages classical concerts year-round (except for July and August). ⓐ Strada Maggiore 43 ⓣ 051 226 807 Ⓝ Bus: 14, 19, 25, 27

Teatro Duse ⓐ Via Cartoleria 42 ⓣ 051 231 836 ⓦ www.teatroduse.it Ⓝ Bus: 16, 30, 39, 59, A, C, E

◑ *Courtyard in Ferrara, dating from 1797*

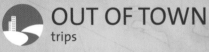

OUT OF TOWN
trips

Parma

Even if you've never heard of the town of Parma, the chances are you've eaten its produce. Parma ham and Parmesan cheese grace the menu of every Italian restaurant the world over, while the Barilla empire, which is now one of the world's biggest pasta producers, also has its roots in the city.

But it's not all about food. The city is one of the great cultural centres of Italy, abounding in impressive architecture, sculptures and artworks, in particular the work of native Mannerist artist Francesco Mazzola, more affectionately known as Parmigianino after his home town. Parma is also renowned as an operatic centre – this was the birthplace, after all, of one of the greatest conductors of all time, Arturo Toscanini.

But, culture aside, simply strolling the medieval streets and dining alfresco in this heartland of Italian cuisine is reason enough to visit.

GETTING THERE

The **Milan–Bologna rail line** (🕿 892 021 (toll free in Italy only) 🌐 www.trenitalia.com) runs through Parma. Forty-eight trains a day arrive from Bologna, and the journey time is one hour to Parma.

Parma's bus and train stations are a 15-minute walk from the central Piazza Garibaldi, or a short ride on buses Nos 8 or 9 (**Parma bus station** 🚌 Piazza della Chiesa 🕿 0521 273 251). **TEP** buses (🚌 Via Taro 12 🕿 0521 2141 🌐 www.tep.pr.it) service the countryside around Parma.

If you're travelling by car, head northwest along the A1 from Bologna. While traffic is not too much of an issue in Parma, finding a parking spot can be a real headache. The five car parks on the outskirts of the city (*parcheggi scambiatori*) are free. You can then

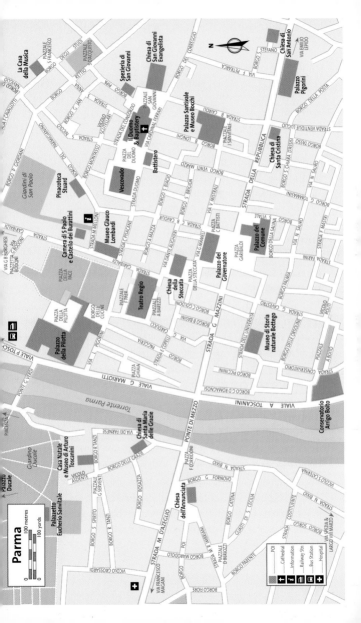

hop on one of the frequent buses (2, 8, 13, 14, 21 or 23) that will bring you to the town centre. There are bus ticket machines in the car parks, and tickets cost about €1.10 each. The city centre is closed to vehicles (except for residents) from 07.30–20.30, so it's really best not to use a car if you can help it.

The main **tourist office** in Parma is ⓐ Strada Melloni 1/A, off the main Strada Garibaldi ⓣ 0521 218 889 ⓦ www.turismo.comune.parma.it ⓛ 09.00–13.00, 15.00–19.00 Mon, 09.00–19.00 Tues–Sat, 09.00–13.00 Sun

SIGHTS & ATTRACTIONS

Chiesa di San Giovanni Evangelista (Church of Saint John the Evangelist)

The most striking feature of this church is the cupola decorated with the 16th-century fresco *Vision of Saint John* by Correggio. Over the door, to the left of the altar, is another painting of Saint John by the same artist. In the chapel are frescoes by Parmigianino. ⓐ Piazzale San Giovanni ⓣ 0521 123 5311 ⓛ 08.30–11.45, 15.00–17.30 Mon–Sat, 15.00–17.45 Sun ⓝ Bus: 7, 8, 11, 23

Il Duomo (Cathedral) & Baptistery

This Romanesque cathedral, built in the 11th century, is one of the most dominant features of the Parma landscape, with its elegant tiered *loggias* looking down over the large square. But to appreciate the true wonders of the building one has to go inside. The main feature is the frescoed cupola depicting *The Assumption* (1526) by Antonio da Correggio, but the cathedral abounds with artworks by this great Renaissance painter and his pupils, including Parmigianino (see page 106).

◆ *The calm cloisters of Chiesa di San Giovanni Evangelista*

Il Duomo in Parma

Also dominating the square is the octagonal Baptistery, looking slightly Moorish in style with its pink marble. It is noted for being an important Italian example of very early Gothic architecture. It is also renowned for Benedetto Antelami's early 13th-century sculptures, which depict the months of the year, the seasons and the signs of the zodiac.

Duomo & Baptistery ⓐ Piazza del Duomo ⓣ 0521 235 886 ⓛ Duomo: 09.00–12.30, 15.00–19.00 daily; Baptistery: 09.00–12.30, 15.00–19.00 daily ⓝ Bus: 7, 8, 11, 23 ⓘ Charge for the Baptistery

Giardino Ducale

Created in the 16th century by the Duke of Parma and Piacenza, in the 18th century Philip II of Bourbon commissioned the redesign of these magnificent gardens along neoclassical lines. In 2001 they were fully restored to this French style. The gardens are also home to the 16th-century Palazzo Ducale and the 15th-century Palazzetto Eucherio Sanvitale. This is now the HQ for the *carabinieri* (high-level police) in Parma. There is also an 18th-century 'little temple', Il Tempietto. ⓦ www.servizi.comune.parma.it/giardinoducale ⓛ 06.00–24.00 daily (Apr–Oct); 07.00–20.00 daily (Nov–Mar)

Palazzo della Pilotta

The one-time home of the powerful Farnese family, who virtually ruled Parma for centuries, was rebuilt after being bombed in World War II and is now home to a variety of important museums and institutions. On the second floor is the Galleria Nazionale (National Gallery), with a comprehensive array of paintings from the 13th century right through to the 19th century. Among the works featured are masterpieces by Correggio, Parmigianino and Canova, as well as *Head of a Young Girl*, attributed to Leonardo da Vinci.

On the ground and first floors of the palace there is the Museo Archeologico Nazionale (National Archaeological Museum), which has an impressive array of finds from several great civilisations, including the ancient Egyptians, Greeks, Etruscans and Romans.

Also on the first floor is the renovated 17th-century Teatro Farnese. This spectacular wooden structure shows clear influence from Palladio with its elegant tiered balconies in neoclassical style. The theatre is particularly important as it was the first in Italy to have (albeit very basic) automated machinery to change sets.

Galleria Nazionale ⓐ Piazzale della Pilotta ❶ 0521 233 309 ⓦ www.gallerianazionaleparma.it ❺ 08.30–13.30 Tues–Sun, closed Mon ⓝ Bus: 1, 6, 7, 8, 9, 10, 11, 12, 13, 15 ❶ Admission charge

Museo Archeologico Nazionale ⓐ Piazzale della Pilotta ❶ 0521 233 718 ❺ 09.30–13.30 Tues–Fri, 09.00–17.30 Sat & Sun, closed Mon (but phone to check as hours vary according to exhibitions) ⓝ Bus: 1, 6, 7, 8, 9, 10, 11, 12, 13, 15 ❶ Admission charge

Teatro Farnese ⓐ Piazzale della Pilotta ❶ 0521 233 309 ❺ 08.30–13.30 Tues–Sun, closed Mon ⓝ Bus: 1, 6, 7, 8, 9, 10, 11, 12, 13, 15 ❶ Admission charge

Piazza Garibaldi

Indisputably the heart of the city ever since Roman times, this square honours two men important to Parma – the great artist Correggio, whose work adorns so many of the churches, and the Italian unifier Garibaldi. Both have statues here.

The two most dominant buildings on the square are the Palazzo del Governatore (Governor's Palace) and the Palazzo del Comune (Town Hall). The former is most notable for its 18th-century bell tower, which can be climbed for wonderful views of the city, and for its sundials on the front of the building. Opposite the

⬡ Statue of Garibaldi in front of the sundial on Piazza Garibaldi

Governor's Palace stands the 17th-century Palazzo del Comune, which is less elaborate in style but is decorated with frescoes on the façade.

Palazzo del Governatore bell tower 🅰 Piazza Garibaldi 17
🛈 0521 212 181 🕒 10.00–12.30, 14.30–16.30 Sat & Sun, closed Mon–Fri
🛈 Maximum eight visitors at a time

Palazzo del Comune 🅰 Strada della Repubblica 1 🛈 0521 2181
🕒 08.30–13.00, 14.30–17.30 Mon & Thur, 08.30–13.00 Tues,
Wed & Fri, closed Sat & Sun Ⓝ Bus: 1, 2, 3, 4, 5, 9, 12, 23

CULTURE

Casa Natale e Museo di Arturo Toscanini (Arturo Toscanini Birthplace and Museum)

The musician and conductor Arturo Toscanini (1867–1957) was born in this house and, although his family moved only a year later, today it is a museum dedicated to his life and work. On display in the individual rooms are items such as his batons, theatre programmes of operas he conducted in Milan, New York and other great cities, as well as personal objects that reflect his family and friendships. 🅰 Borgo R Tanzi 13
🛈 0521 285 499 Ⓦ www.museotoscanini.it 🕒 09.00–13.00, 14.00–18.00
Wed–Sat, 14.00–18.00 Sun, closed Mon & Tues Ⓝ Bus: 2, 6, 21
🛈 No more than 25 people at a time are permitted inside

Teatro Regio

The most important theatre in Parma is its opera house, which opened its doors with a Bellini opera in 1829. Since then it has attracted opera lovers and opera stars from all over the world. The auditorium is fittingly beautiful with its gilded tiered boxes and ceiling and a 19th-century painting of a classical scene on its safety curtain. Every October the Teatro Regio celebrates the month-long Festival Verdi by hosting a

variety of Verdi operas. ⓐ Strada Garibaldi 16A ⓣ 0521 039 393
ⓦ www.teatroregioparma.org ⓛ Tours: 10.30–12.00 Tues–Sat, except
when rehearsals are being held ⓝ Bus: 1, 7, 12 ⓘ Admission charge

RETAIL THERAPY

Antica Salumeria Farini Close to Piazza Garibaldi, this shop stocks a vast
range of cold meats, including Parma ham, and other local delicacies.
You can eat here or buy some of the delicious products, including dried
mushrooms and baby artichokes preserved in olive oil, to take home.
ⓐ Strada Farini 57 ⓣ 0521 234 417 ⓛ 09.00–13.30, 15.30–19.30
Mon–Wed, Fri & Sat, 09.00–13.30 Thur, closed Sun ⓝ Bus: 15

Drogheria Gianfranco Pedrelli Another Aladdin's cave of local produce,
including balsamic vinegar from Modena and a large range of other
goodies. ⓐ Via Spezia 53B ⓣ 0521 253 894 ⓦ www.pedrelli.com
ⓛ 09.00–13.00 Mon–Sat, 16.00–19.30 Mon–Wed, Fri & Sat, closed
Sun ⓝ Bus: 6

Enoteca Fontana The first port of call for wine lovers, this wine merchant
offers bottles from all over the region and often holds tastings, too. The
staff are extremely knowledgeable. ⓐ Strada Farini 24 ⓣ 0521 286 037
ⓛ 09.30–12.30, 16.00–19.30 Tues–Sat, closed Sun ⓝ Bus: 6

Salumeria Garibaldi You can find wedges of Parmesan cheese for sale
on just about every street corner in town, but, if you want to purchase
it in a special setting, this is the place to go. Along with samples, the
friendly staff offer advice on which cheese to buy. ⓐ Strada Garibaldi 42
ⓣ 0521 235 606 ⓦ www.specialitadiparma.it ⓛ 09.00–13.00 Mon–Sat,
16.00–19.30 Mon–Wed, Fri & Sat, closed Sun ⓝ Bus: 1, 2, 15, 23

PARMA CUISINE

The reason that the specialities of the Parma region have become so famous and popular is due to the centuries-old techniques still employed in their production. The hard Parmesan cheese (*parmigiano*) is made with semi-skimmed milk, whey, rennet and salt, then shaped into huge rounds, which can weigh more than 30 kg (66 lb). Its hard texture then lends itself to be sliced, shaved or grated over pasta dishes, although it is also delicious on its own, particularly if accompanied by a glass of local red wine. There are different grades of cheese, depending on how long it has been matured, but the best is *Parmigiano Reggiano*. The whey that is separated from the curds is then used to feed the pigs. These in turn give the town its other great product: cured Parma ham (*prosciutto*).

AFTER DARK

RESTAURANTS

Trattoria dei Corrieri £–££ Regional cuisine at reasonable prices. *Tortellini* with cream and ravioli stuffed with braised beef are among the dishes served by the attentive staff in this popular restaurant.
ⓐ Strada Conservatorio 1 ⓣ 0521 234 426 ⓦ www.trattoriacorrieri.it
ⓛ 12.30–14.30, 19.30–22.30 daily ⓥ Bus: 12, 13, 15, 21

Gallo d'Oro ££ Do not be put off by the slightly dated décor – the food is fresh and delicious and locals have been flocking here for years. Try the *salumi misti* made with locally cured hams, and the roasted lamb stuffed with bread, cheese and eggs. ⓐ Borgo della

Salina 3 ☎ 0521 208 846 ⏰ 12.00–15.00, 19.00–02.00 Mon–Sat, closed Sun 🚌 Bus: 1, 3, 4, 5, 6, 9, 11

Parizzi ££ Housed in a gorgeous building that dates from the mid-16th century, this excellent *trattoria* has been run by the same family since 1958. Under the skylit patio you can enjoy dishes such as *culatelo* (cured ham made from the haunches of wild boar) or a Parmesan soufflé with white truffles. Or try the roasted guinea fowl with Fonseca wine prepared by the famous Marco Parizzi himself, a celebrated television chef, appearing on the Italian equivalent of *Ready, Steady, Cook!*
🏠 Strada della Repubblica 71 ☎ 0521 285 952
🌐 www.ristoranteparizzi.it ⏰ 12.30–14.30, 19.30–22.30 Tues–Sat, closed Sun & Mon 🚌 Bus: 3, 4, 5, 23

CLUBS, CINEMA & THEATRE
For some lively after-dinner nightlife, try **Dadaumpa** (🏠 Via Emilio Lepido 48 ☎ 0521 483 802 🌐 www.dadaumpa.com) or **The Kitchen** (🏠 Via Mazzini 1 ☎ 0521 386 188). Parma has an excellent range of cinemas, including – for serious cinephiles – **Fondazione Culturale Solares** (🏠 Largo VIII Marzo 33 ☎ 0521 967 088). There are also four theatres, including the historic **Teatro Regio** (see page 114), which stages opera and ballet and is home to the annual Verdi Festival.

ACCOMMODATION

Much like Bologna, Parma doesn't really cater to budget travellers, although there are cheaper accommodation options near the railway and bus stations.

● *Piazza Garibaldi*

HOTELS

Leon d'Oro £–££ This is an option only if you're really on a shoestring budget. Almost all of the rooms share communal bathroom facilities (just two have en-suite facilities), and there are six flights of stairs with no lift. It's also on a noisy street near the station. ❸ Via Fratti 4 ❶ 0521 773 182 Ⓝ Bus: 7, 11, 13, 14

Albergo Brenta ££ A pleasant, good-value place to stay in the centre – quite a rarity at this location. Family run, and clean, but don't expect any mod cons, although all rooms are en-suite. ❸ Via G B Borghesi 12 ❶ 0521 208 093 Ⓦ www.hotelbrenta.it Ⓝ Bus: 1, 3, 4, 5, 6, 9, 11

Park Hotel Stendhal £££ Located in the historic centre, this comfortable and popular refurbished hotel overlooks the green space of the Piazza della Pace. ❸ Piazzetta Bodoni 3 ❶ 0521 208 057

Starhotel du Parc £££ A sumptuously furnished hotel in the historic centre overlooking the beautiful Giardino Ducale (Ducal Park). There is an excellent restaurant serving modern international and traditional Italian cuisine. ❸ Viale Piacenza 12C ❶ 0521 292 929 Ⓦ www.starhotels.it Ⓝ Bus: 9, 12, 19

B&B

B&B Rubra £–££ Run by a friendly young couple, this renovated home with a garden area is situated across the river from the city's old town, though it's an easy walk into the centre. Facilities include free use of bicycles and Internet. ❸ Strada M d'Azeglio 48 ❶ 0521 289 140 Ⓦ www.bbrubra.com Ⓝ Bus: 3, 4, 5, 23

Ravenna

Ravenna's very existence is due to its proximity to Classe, an important port during the Roman period that at one time served as the capital of the western Roman Empire because of its defensible position. By 476, however, the western Empire had fallen and Ravenna came under the rule of the Christian Ostrogoths. Two hundred years later the Byzantines took control, and it was these two periods that produced the outpourings of artistic creativity that have made Ravenna such a popular destination for visitors to this day. Both the Goths and the Byzantines, wanting to appear powerful and influential, decorated lavishly. The remnants of their stunning mosaics, particularly in San Vitale, still excite admiration. They have also earned Ravenna UNESCO World Heritage Site status.

Ravenna is a small town. Most of the sights, shops, restaurants and accommodation are within easy walking distance of each other. Its relaxed atmosphere lends itself to quiet strolls and café lunches, although it does come alive during the annual **Ravenna Music Festival** each June and July (❶ 0544 249 244 ❾ www.ravennafestival.org). Opera greats such as the late Luciano Pavarotti have performed here in the past. The Dante Festival, or Settembre Dantesco, during which readings of the *Divine Comedy* (*Divina Commedia*) take place, is sponsored by the church of San Francesco and held during the second week of September.

GETTING THERE

Ravenna is 80 km (50 miles) from Bologna. There is a frequent rail service from Bologna, and the one-hour journey time makes it an easy day trip from the region's main city. Ravenna's train station,

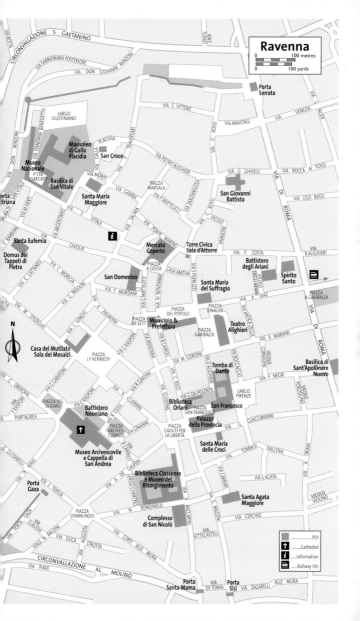

Stazione Centrale (ⓐ Piazza Farini Carlo Luigi 13 ⓣ 0544 212 755), is a ten-minute walk from the city centre. There is also a frequent service from Ferrara, which connects through Venice. For train information and schedules, call Trenitalia (see page 54).

By car from Bologna, head east along the A14; if coming from Ferrara, take the SS16. Bear in mind that most of the city centre is closed to vehicles of non-residents. If you are arriving by car, it's best to leave your vehicle in one of the 11 car parks clearly signposted around the city. The city centre is small, and it is served by an extensive network of buses – see ⓦ www.atm.ra.it for further details.

The English-speaking staff at the **tourist office** (ⓐ Via Salara 8 ⓣ 0544 357 55 or 354 04 ⓦ www.turismo.ravenna.it) are friendly and knowledgeable. Stop in here for maps, information about bicycle hire (a good way to get around), and a combination ticket to the city's attractions. There are 40 yellow bicycles that can be used, free of charge, by visiting tourists. Staff at the tourist office will guide you through the registration necessary in order to do so.

SIGHTS & ATTRACTIONS

The Baptisteries

There are two octagonal baptisteries in Ravenna that are noted for their mosaics, which depict the Baptism of Christ, surrounded by his 12 Apostles. The Battistero Neoniano is considered to be the oldest-surviving religious building in Ravenna (5th century), although the Battistero degli Ariani is only about half a century younger. Both are now UNESCO World Heritage Sites.

Battistero Neoniano ⓐ Piazza del Duomo ⓣ 0544 541 688 ⓦ www.ravennamosaici.it ⓛ daily 09.00–19.00 (Apr–Sept);

09.30–17.30 (Mar & Oct); 10.00–17.00 (Nov–Feb) Ⓝ Bus: Metrobus Giallo, Metrobus Rosso A, 2, 3, 4, 5 ❶ Admission charge

Battistero degli Ariani ⓐ Vicolo degli Ariani ❶ 0544 543 711 ❶ 08.30–19.30 daily Ⓝ Bus: 2, 3, 5

Basilica di Sant'Apollinare Nuovo

A 6th-century church that contains some of the finest mosaics in Ravenna, depicting events from the life of Christ as well as images of the prophets and the Apostles. Outside, adjacent to the porticoed façade, there is a 10th-century stone bell tower. ⓐ Piazza Arcivescovile 1 ❶ 0544 541 688 Ⓦ www.ravennamosaici.it ❶ daily 09.00–19.00 (Apr–Sept); 09.30–17.30 (Mar & Oct); 10.00–17.00 (Nov–Feb) Ⓝ Bus: Metrobus Giallo, Metrobus Rosso A, 3, 4, 5 ❶ Admission charge

Basilica di San Vitale

The focal point of any visit to Ravenna is the Church of San Vitale. Stepping into the gloomy exterior from the bright sunlight outside does not immediately do its treasures justice, but once your eyes have adjusted you are met with a quite extraordinary sight – dazzling gold and glass mosaics dating from the 5th century AD. Even more fascinating is that these mosaics survive not only as some of the last great works of art of the ancient world, but also as one of Christianity's first. Building of the church began in 525 during the reign of Theodoric the Ostrogoth – by the time it was finished, 23 years later, Ravenna was in the hands of the Byzantine emperor, Justinian. Indeed, it is thought that San Vitale provided the inspiration for the masterful Hagia Sofia in Istanbul.

Based on two concentric octagons, the central dome is supported by eight columns, with recesses emanating from each side. In one of these recesses is the breathtaking semicircular apse covered with an

intricate gold mosaic, depicting Christ with San Vitale. The archbishop of Ravenna and Emperor Justinian are also heavily featured, as is Theodora, an Evita-esque figure of the Byzantine Empire who progressed from dancing girl to empress through feminine guile. Daylight streaming in from the arched windows only adds to the glow of the mosaics here.

The choir area, too, has some spectacular mosaic work, this time deviating from the usual gold colour scheme to bring in the greens and blues of nature and the multicoloured plumage of birds. There are also biblical scenes from the Old and New Testaments, with mosaics depicting Abraham and Christ's Apostles, among other things. In front of the choir is a mosaic maze on the floor, which was a fairly standard addition in Roman times.

Aside from the mosaics – as if there needed to be any more attractions – other features of the church include walls covered in a thin sheet of precious marbles from all over the Mediterranean, an altar dating from the 6th century, ancient reliefs of the *Throne of Neptune* and the *Sacrifice of Isaac* near the choir, and the sarcophagus of Quintus Bonus, complete with reliefs of the Magi and of Daniel in the lions' den. ➋ Via Fiandrini Benedetto ❶ 0544 541 688 ⓦ www.ravennamosaici.it ❷ daily 09.00–19.00 (Apr–Sept); 09.00–17.30 (Mar & Oct); 09.30–17.00 (Nov–Feb) ✿ Bus: 1 ❶ Admission charge

Mausoleo di Galla Placidia (Galla Placidia's Mausoleum)

Built in a cross shape between AD 425 and 433, the mausoleum houses the oldest of Ravenna's mosaics; these are exceptionally vivid, utlilising peacock blue, moss green, gold, deep purple and burnt orange. It's certainly elaborate for a burial place of one of the most controversial women in Roman history. Galla Placidia was the sister of Honorius, one of Rome's last emperors. When the Goths sacked Rome, Galla was

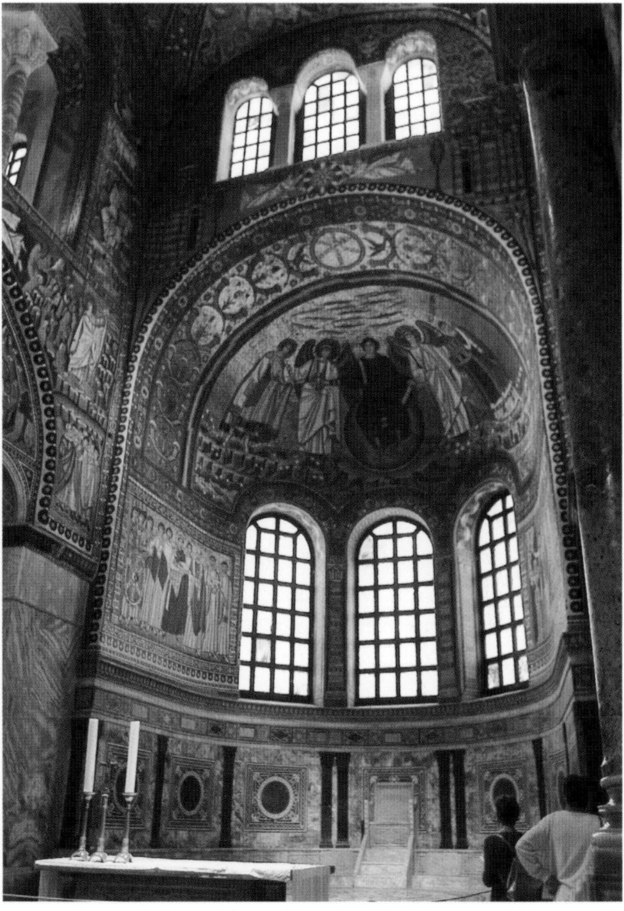

A side altar in the Basilica di San Vitale

TOMBA DI DANTE (DANTE'S TOMB)

Italy's finest poet, Dante Alighieri, was exiled from his native Florence as the rivalries between the Vatican and the Holy Roman Empire were being waged, and he died in Ravenna in September 1321, not long after completing the third part of his magnificent *Divine Comedy* trilogy: *Paradiso*. Given his revered status in Italy, his tomb is surprisingly simple, its lamp kept alight by oil donated from Florence. Near the tomb is the 5th-century church of San Francesco, where Dante's funeral took place, and on the first floor is the **Museo Dantesco** (② Via Dante Alighieri 4), which has a collection of paintings, sculptures and books connected to the poet. ⓐ Bus: Metrobus Giallo, Metrobus Rosso A, 1, 3, 4, 5

● *Visit the tomb of one of Italy's most revered poets, Dante*

taken hostage – then scandalously married one of her kidnappers, Ataulf. She battled beside him as they headed south, reigning jointly with him over the Gothic kingdom. When her husband was killed she returned to the Romans, married a Roman general, Constantius, and bore him a son, who became the emperor Valentinian III at the age of six, as his regent Galla took control of the western Roman Empire. She eventually died in Rome in AD 450 but, having given much funding to Ravenna's churches during her lifetime, she is honoured here with this impressive tomb. ⓐ Via Don Giovanni Minzoni ① 0544 541 688 ⓦ www.ravennamosaici.it ⓛ daily 09.00–19.00 (Apr–Sept); 09.00–17.30 (Mar & Oct); 09.30–17.00 (Nov–Feb) ⓝ Bus: 1 ① Admission charge

Piazza del Popolo

During the Byzantine period Venice became a great world power and briefly ruled a large part of Italy, including Ravenna, during which time the Venetians built this square. They governed from the mid-15th-century Palazzetta Veneziana and oversaw the construction of the two towers honouring the town's patron saints, San Vitale and Sant'Apollinare.

North of Piazza del Popolo on Via Ponte Marino is Ravenna's medieval leaning tower, the 12th-century Torre Civica Sala d'Attorre, which is now supported by steel struts. ⓝ Bus: Metrobus Giallo, Metrobus Rosso A, 1, 3, 4, 5

CULTURE

Museo Arcivescovile e Cappella di San Andrea (Archiepiscopal Museum and Chapel of San Andrea)

Ravenna's Archbishop's Palace was built in the 6th century under the guidance of Archbishop Maximian, and the main attraction here is his ivory throne. In the chapel of San Andrea are yet more mosaics,

notable not just for their design and colours, but for the rather shocking image of Christ as a warrior. This step away from his traditionally peaceful image possibly reflects the troubled times that existed during the construction of the work. ⓐ Piazza Arcivescovado ⓣ 0544 541 688 ⓦ www.ravennamosaici.it ⓛ daily 09.00–19.00 (Apr–Sept); 09.00–17.30 (Mar & Oct); 09.30–17.00 (Nov–Feb) ⓝ Bus: Metrobus Giallo, Metrobus Rosso A, 2, 3, 4, 5 ⓘ Admission charge

Museo Nazionale (National Museum)

The early Christian and Byzantine eras were so important to Ravenna that this museum is certainly not to be missed if you want to understand the period. Among the archaeological objects housed here dating from that time are paintings, tapestries, burial items, weaponry and much more, giving you good insight into Ravenna's history. ⓐ Via Fiandrini Benedetto ⓣ 0544 543 711 ⓛ 09.00–18.00 Mon–Sat, closed Sun ⓝ Bus: 1 ⓘ Admission charge

RETAIL THERAPY

Studio Akomena Since Ravenna is best known for its mosaics, buying a replica makes for the ideal souvenir. Here you'll find all manner of religious copies in the traditional golden hues. ⓐ Via Ponte Delle Vecchia 27 ⓣ 0544 554 700 ⓛ 09.00–19.00 Mon–Sat, closed Sun ⓝ Bus: 3, 10, 11

AFTER DARK

Ristorante La Gardela ££–£££ A lovely traditional restaurant near most of Ravenna's main sights. The speciality here is *tortelloni della casa* – pasta served with cream, spinach, tomatoes and herbs. Or try the *ravioli* stuffed with truffles, or *tagliatelle* with porcini mushrooms. There's also a good wine list. ❷ Via Ponte Marino 3 ❶ 0544 217 147 ● 12.00–14.30, 19.00–22.00 Fri–Wed, closed Thur

ACCOMMODATION

Accommodation in Ravenna, as in the rest of the region, is not cheap on the whole; however, there is one hostel and a few bed and breakfasts that offer simple but clean options.

Ostello Dante £ Situated east of the train station, this place fills up fast in summer, so book ahead if you're on a tight budget. ❷ Via Nicolodi 12 ❶ 0544 421 164 Ⓝ Bus: 1, 70, 80 from outside the train station

Hotel Centrale Byron £–££ Nicely decorated in Art Deco style and benefiting from a very central location, just a few steps from Piazza del Popolo. ❸ Via IV Novembre 14 ❶ 0544 33 479 Ⓦ www.hotelbyron.com Ⓝ 5 mins from the railway station

Hotel Argentario ££ Situated near the historic centre and the railway station, this is a comfortable hotel. Rooms have en-suite bathrooms, minibars and air conditioning, and a buffet breakfast is included. ❷ Via di Roma 45 ❶ 0544 36 926 Ⓦ www.hotelargentarioravenna.it Ⓝ Bus: Metrobus Giallo, Metrobus Rosso A, 3, 4, 5

NH Hotel £££ This is a modern, comfortable and conveniently situated hotel with friendly staff, bright and airy public areas and lifts. There is a bar and restaurant; an excellent buffet breakfast is included in the price. ❷ Piazza Mameli 1 ❶ 0544 357 62 Ⓦ www.nh-hotels.com Ⓝ Bus: 2, 3, 5

Ferrara

The strongest influence on the landscape of Ferrara was the powerful d'Este family, who ruled the town from the 13th to the 16th centuries, during the height of the Renaissance. The city walls, which they constructed, still stand, and the works of the 15th-century artists of the Ferrara School, including Cosme Tura, Ercole de'Roberti, Lorenzo Costa and Francesco del Cossa, are among the main attractions for visitors today. Poets were also patronised by the d'Este family and produced three of the Italian Renaissance's greatest works: Boiardo's *Orlando Innamorato* in 1483, Ariosto's better-known continuation of the same story *Orlando Furioso* in 1532 and Tasso's *Gerusalemme Liberata* in 1581. Today the city is one of the best preserved in terms of Renaissance architecture and is ideal for strolling around.

Ferrara's Palio di San Giorgio – dating from the 13th century and the oldest in the world – is a local highlight. It is held in the Piazza Ariostea on the last Sunday of May (see page 14).

Some excellent jazz and classical concerts are the main events of the **Ferrara sotto le Stelle** (W www.ferrarasottolestelle.it), an outdoor festival that runs from late June until early July. In August is the **Ferrara Buskers' Festival** (W www.ferrarabuskers.com), in which street musicians from all over the world descend on the town to play and sing for the locals and visitors.

GETTING THERE

Ferrara is around 50 km (30 miles) northeast of Bologna. If travelling from Bologna by car, take the A13 north. Ferrara is situated on the main railway line from Bologna to Padua and Venice, and there are frequent trains. The rail journey time from Bologna to Ferrara is only

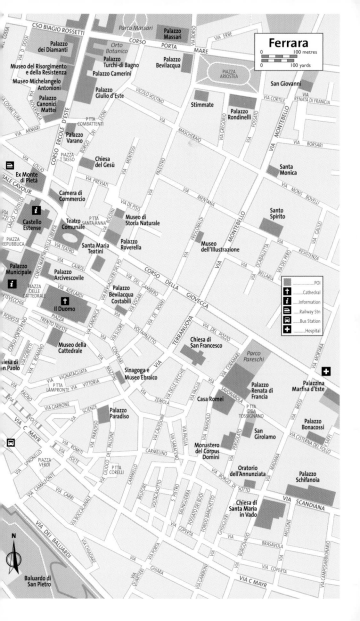

Ferrara

| 0 | 100 metres |
| 0 | 100 yards |

CSO BIAGIO ROSSETTI

Parco Massari

Palazzo dei Diamanti

CORSO PORTA MARE

VIA ERBE

VIA BORSO

Palazzo Massari

Museo del Risorgimento e della Resistenza

Museo Michelangelo Antonioni

Orto Botanico

Palazzo Turchi-di Bagno

Palazzo Camerini

Palazzo Bevilacqua

PIAZZA ARIOSTEA

San Giovanni

VIA RENATA DI FRANCIA

Palazzo Canonici Mattei

Palazzo Giulio d'Este

VICOLO VOLTINO

VIA CORTILE

VIA ARMARI

P.TTA DE' LEON COMBATTENTI

Stimmate

Palazzo Rondinelli

VIA MONTEBELLO

VIA BORSARI

VIA COSMETURA

Palazzo Varano

VIA MASCHERAIO

VIA GREGORIO

VIA LOLLIO

CORSO ERCOLE D'ESTE

PIAZZA T.TASSO

Chiesa del Gesù

VIA MENTESSI

VIA PALESTRO

Santa Monica

VIA MONS. BOVELLI

VIALE CAVOUR

Ex Monte di Pietà

VIA PREVIATI

VIA DE PISIS

VIA MENTANA

Santo Spirito

VIA CALTELI

VIA CASTELLO

VIA TARGAT CASTELLO

Camera di Commercio

P.TTA SANT'ANNA

Museo di Storia Naturale

VIA FRESCOBALDI

VIA MONTEBELLO

VIA RESISTENZA

PIAZZA REPUBBLICA

Castello Estense

Teatro Comunale

Santa Maria Teatini

Palazzo Roverella

Museo dell'Illustrazione

VIA VOLTACASOTTO

VIA BELLARIA

VIA DEL PIRO

Palazzo Municipale

CORSO MARTIRI DELLA LIBERTÀ

Palazzo Arcivescovile

VIA CAIROLI

Palazzo Bevilacqua Costabili

CORSO DELLA GIOVECCA

VIA DEL CAMBERO

VIA TEATRO

VIA ADELARDI

PIAZZA DELLE CATTEDRALE

Il Duomo

VIA DE ROMEI

TERRANUOVA

VIA DEL POZZO

PONTE CASTELLO

PIAZZA TRENTO TRIESTE

VIA CANONICA

VIA SIORE

VOLTAPALETTO

Chiesa di San Francesco

Parco Pareschi

CORSO PORTA RENO

Museo della Cattedrale

VIA CONTRARI

Palazzina Marfisa d'Este

Chiesa di San Paolo

VIA CAIRELLI

VIA MAZZINI

Sinagoga e Museo Ebraico

Palazzo Renata di Francia

VIA BAGNO

P.TTA LAMPRONTE

VIA VIGNATAGLIATA

VIA VITTORIA

VIA DELLE VECCHIE

Casa Romei

VIA SAVONAROLA

Palazzo Bonacossi

VIA C. MAYR

PIAZZA VERDI

SCIENZE

Palazzo Paradiso

VIA PRAISOLO

P.TTA G.DA TOSSIGNANO

San Girolamo

VIA CISTERNA DEL FOLLO

VIA SIRONI LO

VIA ROMITI

VIA VOLTE

CARMELINO

VIA SARACENO

Monastero del Corpus Domini

VIA MADAMA

VIA CAMALEONTE

VIA CARRI

VIA GIUOCO DEL PALLONE

VIA CAMMELLO

VIA BORGO DI SOTTO

Oratorio dell'Annunziata

Palazzo Schifanoia

VIA DEL BALUARDI

VIA BROCCAINDOSSO

VIA CHIODAIA

P.TTA CORELLI

BELFIORE

VOLTAGATTO

S. PIETRO

SALINGUERRA

FONDO BANCHETTO

GHISILIERI

VIA SCANDIANA

Chiesa di Santa Maria in Vado

N

VIA QUARTIERI

VIA PORTA

ROSSETTO DI BUOI

FONDO BANCHETTO

VIA GHIARA

VIA BORGO

BRASAVOLA

VIA COPERTA

VIA C. MAYR

Baluardo di San Pietro

VIA MELLONE

VIA CAMPOSABBIONARIO

Legend:
- POI
- ✝ Cathedral
- ℹ Information
- 🚃 Railway Stn
- 🚌 Bus Station
- ✚ Hospital

◆ *Castello Estense*

30 minutes, making it an easy day trip from the city. Ferrara's train station is west of the city walls, a 15-minute walk along Viale Cavour to the centre of town, or a ride on bus 1, 6, 9, 10 and 11. For information and train schedules, call Trenitalia (see page 54). There is a general public transport website ⓦ www.ami.fe.it

The main **tourist office** is at Castello Estense (ⓐ Piazza del Castello Estense ⓣ 0532 209 370 ⓦ www.ferraraterraeacqua.it ⓝ Bus: 1, 2, 4, 9). From here, you can pick up free maps and get advice on accommodation.

SIGHTS & ATTRACTIONS

Castello Estense

The d'Este family may have been powerful, but they certainly weren't popular among Ferrara's over-taxed citizens, so the wide moat surrounding their dynastic home was probably a necessity rather than a design feature.

The castle was commissioned by Nicolò II, who began construction on 29 September 1385 and ended up with a striking, fortress-style edifice dominating the town with its imposing towers. His son, Nicolò III, was the man largely responsible for its interior style. A tyrant in his personal life (he ordered the assassination of his first wife when he discovered she was having an affair), he was nevertheless an avid patron of the arts, and his taste is reflected in the décor.

Much of the castle is now occupied by office space, but there are a few rooms that have been preserved to illustrate the d'Estes' presence here, including the Salone dei Giochi (Games Room), decorated with frescoes by Sebastiano Filippi, depicting sports popular at the time such as discus-throwing, chariot-racing and wrestling. ⓐ Largo Castello ⓣ 0532 299 233 ⓦ www.castelloestense.it ⓛ 09.30–17.30 Tues–Sun

(June–Feb); 09.30–17.30 Tues–Sun (Mar–May), closed Mon Bus: 1, 3C, 4C, 8, 9, 10, 11 ❶ Admission charge

City walls

Ferrara's impressive medieval walls surround the city for 9 km (5½ miles), punctuated at certain points by bastions, gateways and towers. They were built at the instigation of Alfonso I in order to protect the d'Este dynasty. When the family was banished to Modena by the pope in 1598, however, it was exactly these same walls through which they had to depart their city. Today the walls offer great views of both the city and the surrounding landscape, and make an ideal location for cycling or picnicking.

Il Duomo

Opposite the Palazzo Municipale is the magnificent 12th-century cathedral that is designed in a striking combination of Gothic and Romanesque styles. Its façade dominates the square, with its triple roofs and tiered *loggias* and bas-reliefs illustrating the Last Judgement. The statue in the alcove over the main door is a sculpture of Saint George by Nicholaus. The unfinished *campanile* (bell tower) was designed by Leon Battista Alberti. In constrast to the façade, the interior is more Baroque in style. There's also a museum attached to the cathedral that contains artworks dating from the 15th century as well as various marble sculptures. ⓐ Piazza delle Cattedrale ❶ 0532 207 449 ❶ 07.30–12.00, 15.00–18.30 Mon–Sat, 07.30–12.30, 15.30–19.30 Sun ⓝ Bus: 2, 3C

Palazzo dei Diamanti

For art lovers, the best place to see works of artists of the Ferrara School is in the Pinocoteca Nazionale (National Gallery) in the Palazzo dei

Diamanti (Diamond Palace), so named because its exterior stone decorations are carved in the shape of diamond points. Inside are works by Cosme Tura, Francesco del Cossa and Lorenzo Costa, among others. There's also a gallery of modern art here, with paintings by artists such as Gauguin and Klimt. ❷ Corso Ercole d'Este 21 ❶ 0532 244 949 ◔ 09.00–14.00 Tues, Wed, Fri & Sat, 09.00–19.00 Thur, 09.00–13.00 Sun, closed Mon ❽ Bus: 3C, 4C ❶ Admission charge

Palazzo Municipale

South of the Castello Estense is the Palazzo Municipale (Town Hall), which was built in 1243, soon after Azzo d'Este seized control of the city. Given its age and importance, restoration work is ongoing, so it is not always open to the public. Its main attraction is in any case its façade, particularly the bronze statues of Nicolò III on horseback and his son and heir, Borso, sitting on his throne. ❷ Corso Martiri della Libertà ❽ Bus: 2, 3C, 4C

● *Il Duomo and Museo Cattedrale*

Palazzo Schifanoia

The Schifanoia Palace was built in 1385 by Albert V d'Este and was enlarged by Borso d'Este from 1450 to 1471. The family used this rather than the Castello Estense as their summer residence. The main interest for visitors today is the Salone dei Mesi (Room of the Months), where masterful murals illustrate the 12 months of the year. Each month is subdivided into three horizontal bands: the lower band shows scenes from everyday life in the town at that time of year, the middle shows the relative sign of the zodiac, and the upper depicts the classical god assigned to the month. The works are generally attributed to Cosme Tura, the official court painter who founded the Ferrarese School of art.

Also in the *palazzo* is the Civic Museum of Ancient Art, which displays, among other things, ancient coins, bronzes and Renaissance plates and pottery. ⓐ Via Scandiana 23 ⓣ 0532 244 949 ⓛ 09.00–18.00 Tues–Sun, closed Mon ⓝ Bus: 1, 9 ⓘ Admission charge

RETAIL THERAPY

Ceramiche Artistiche Ferraresi A wonderful shop selling locally crafted and brightly decorated ceramics, making ideal gifts or souvenirs. ⓐ Via Pomatelli 11 ⓣ 0532 762 200 ⓛ 10.00–19.00 Mon–Sat, closed Sun ⓝ Bus: 3C, 4C

AFTER DARK

Max £–££ There's a student atmosphere here; all come to enjoy the relaxed ambience and the extensive wine list. ⓐ Piazza delle Repubblica 16 ⓣ 0544 209 309 ⓛ 12.30–14.30, 19.30–22.30 Tues–Sun, closed Mon ⓝ Bus: 1, 9

PIAZZA TRENTO – GENIUS FOR SALE

Ferrara hosts a variety of markets over the course of every month. Visit the first weekend of every month (09.00–19.00 Sat & Sun, Sept–July) to pick up everything from second-hand furniture to antique chandeliers. On the third weekend of each month (09.00–19.00 Sat & Sun, Sept–Nov & Jan–July), the same spot hosts stalls of artisan craftworks. And on the final Sunday of the month (09.00–19.00 Sept–July), in a market modestly entitled 'Genius Creations', individuals pile in with eccentric, often home-made, items. ⓦ Bus: 3C, 4C, 11

La Provvidenza £££ A wonderfully romantic dinner option, particularly in warm weather when you can dine outside as the sun goes down. Portions of dishes such as *fettucine* with smoked salmon are very large, so if you like dessert, it might be best to forgo a starter. ⓐ Corso Ercole I d'Este 92 ⓣ 0544 205 187 ⓛ 12.00–15.30, 19.30–22.30 Tues–Sun, closed Mon ⓝ Bus: 3, 9 ⓘ Reservations recommended

ACCOMMODATION

There are a number of affordable hotels in Ferrara, most of them near the city centre.

HOTELS

Hotel Europa ££ A good-value city-centre option with friendly staff and en-suite rooms. An added advantage is that it offers parking facilities for a minimal extra charge. ⓐ Corso della Giovecca 49 ⓣ 0544 205 456 ⓦ www.hoteleuropaferrara.com ⓝ Bus: 9

Locanda Borgonuovo ££ This elegant bed and breakfast is set in a 17th-century former monastery near Castello Estense. The large rooms are elegantly decorated with antiques and are all en-suite. Breakfast is included and is served in the garden in warm weather. ⓐ Via Cairoli 29 ⓣ 0544 211 100 ⓦ www.borgonuovo.com ⓝ Bus: 1, 9 ⓘ Reservations strongly recommended

Hotel Annunziata £££ A lovely hotel that mixes sharp modern décor with 17th-century beams, located directly opposite the Castello Estense (there are also suites in a separate 13th-century building in the grounds of the hotel). Buffet breakfast is included in the price. ⓐ Piazza Repubblica 5 ⓣ 0544 201 111 ⓦ www.annunziata.it ⓝ Bus: 1, 3C, 4C, 8, 9, 10, 11

HOSTEL
Student's Hostel Estense Northwest of the city centre, the rooms are unusually large here and very clean, but all bathroom facilities are shared. The reception is always open and there is 24-hour check-in ⓐ Corso Biagio Rossetti 24 ⓣ 0532 201 158 ⓦ www.ostelloferrara.it ⓝ Bus: 3C

◗ *A train waits at Bologna's Stazione Centrale*

PRACTICAL
information

Directory

GETTING THERE
By air

If Bologna is the only place you will be visiting on your trip, travelling there by air is usually the most cost-effective way to go, particularly as it is now served from the UK by low-cost airlines. Fares will depend on what season you choose to travel, the highest being at Easter, during the Festa di San Luca in May (see page 65), any time between June to mid-August and Christmas to New Year. Prices are considerably lower during the seasons of September to October and November to March, when the city is also considerably less crowded. Weekend trips are usually around ten per cent more expensive than weekday air fares.

The low-cost airline Ryanair offers fares that can range from around £20 (if booked early enough) to £100 from London Stansted to Forlì airport, which is about 80 km (50 miles) from Bologna. There's a one-hour train ride to the city or a 1½-hour bus trip. There are also frequent flights on British Airways to Bologna from London Gatwick. Bologna is also connected by direct flights to many European cities, including Amsterdam, Barcelona, Brussels, Copenhagen, Frankfurt, Lyon, Lisbon, Madrid, Nice, Paris, Vienna and Zurich. Aer Lingus operates flights from Dublin to Bologna.

Try these online booking sites:

Expedia Ⓦ www.expedia.co.uk
Orbitz Ⓦ www.orbitz.com
Priceline Ⓦ www.priceline.com
Travelocity Ⓦ www.travelocity.com

Some of the major airlines flying to Bologna are:
Aer Lingus ❶ 02 4345 8326 Ⓦ www.aerlingus.com

◆ *Neptune fountain, Piazza Maggiore – the picture every visitor takes*

Alitalia ☎ 06 2222 Ⓦ www.alitalia.com
British Airways ☎ 199 71 22 66 Ⓦ www.britishairways.com
Ryanair ☎ 899 67 89 10 Ⓦ www.ryanair.com

Many people are aware that air travel emits CO_2, which contributes to climate change. You may be interested in the possibility of lessening the environmental impact of your flight through the charity **Climate Care** (Ⓦ www.jpmorganclimatecare.com), which offsets your CO_2 by funding environmental projects around the world.

By rail

The easiest way to take the train to Bologna from the UK is by Eurostar from London St Pancras International to Paris, then take a train from Paris to Milan, and again from Milan to Bologna. The journey time is approximately 18–20 hours. Relevant companies include:

Eurail Ⓦ www.eurail.com
Eurostar ☎ 0870 518 6186 or 0044 1233 617 575 Ⓦ www.eurostar.co.uk
InterRail ☎ 0870 084 1411 Ⓦ www.interrailnet.com
Rail Europe ☎ 08448 484 064 Ⓦ www.raileurope.co.uk

The Europe-wide InterRail and Eurail passes give unlimited travel on the Italian national train network.

The monthly **Thomas Cook European Rail Timetable** (☎ (UK) 01733 416477, (USA) 1 800 322 3834 Ⓦ www.thomascookpublishing.com) has up-to-date schedules for European international and national train services.

By road

If you're really on a shoestring budget, National Express does offer overland European coach services, but it's not recommended unless you're touring Europe as a whole. The journey time between London and Bologna is around 36 long, boring hours.

National Express Eurolines 📞 08705 143219 🌐 www.eurolines.co.uk

The main motorway (*autostrada*) into Bologna is the A1, which comes south from eastern France and through Milan and Parma.

You must be over 18 years of age to drive a car in Italy and have a valid driving licence. Driving is on the right-hand side of the road.

ENTRY FORMALITIES

British citizens need a valid passport to enter Italy. All other European Union (EU) citizens can enter the country by producing either a valid passport or a national identity card. All EU citizens may stay in the country for as long as they wish. Citizens of the United States, Canada, Australia and New Zealand need a valid passport, but are limited to stays of three months. All other nationals should consult the relevant embassies (see page 155) about requirements.

In terms of carriage of goods, there are almost no restrictions on what legal goods can be imported or exported to and from other EU countries, as long as you can prove that they are for your own use and not for resale. Large quantities of any item are likely to excite suspicion. To import tobacco or alcohol you must be over the age of 17.

For visitors from outside the EU, the restrictions on importing are as follows:

400 cigarettes; or 100 cigarillos; or 50 cigars; or 250 g of tobacco

60 cc of perfume

2 litres of still table wine

250 cc of eau de toilette

1 litre of spirits or strong liqueurs over 22 per cent volume; or 2 litres of fortified wine, sparkling wine or other liqueurs

£145 worth of all other goods including gifts and souvenirs.

⬢ *Bologna, city of arcades*

MONEY

Italy's currency is the euro (€), and notes are issued in denominations of 5, 10, 20, 50, 100, 200 and 500 euros. Coins are issued in denominations of 1, 2, 5, 10, 20 and 50 cents and 1 and 2 euros.

The easiest way to obtain euros is from ATMs (cash machines), located at the airport and throughout the city. They accept all major credit cards and debit cards bearing the Maestro and Cirrus symbols. You can buy euro notes ahead of your trip from banks and bureaux de change in your home country and you can also exchange currency in Bologna. Beware the low exchange rates or high commission fees of some bureaux de change. Bologna's main bank branches are along Via dell'Indipendenza, Via Rizzoli and Via Ugo Bassi. They are generally open 08.30–13.30 and 14.30–15.30 on weekdays, and closed at weekends. Most of the major credit cards are accepted in all but the smallest of restaurants and shops, but do make sure you carry some cash with you.

It's always good to have some traveller's cheques on hand when you travel. Try to get them in different denominations, and keep the purchase agreement and a record of the cheques' serial numbers in a different place from the actual cheques. The most widely accepted traveller's cheques are **Thomas Cook** (Ⓦ www.thomascook.com) and **American Express** (Ⓦ www.americanexpress.com). If the cheques are lost or stolen, be sure to report it immediately to the issuing company. In most cases the cheques will be replaced within 24 hours.

On euro traveller's cheques you should not have to pay any commission when exchanging them for euros. For other currency cheques there is usually a commission charge of one per cent of the amount changed. Both Thomas Cook and American Express sell euro traveller's cheques.

HEALTH, SAFETY & CRIME

The European Health Insurance Card (EHIC), valid for five years, has replaced the E111 form for UK travellers using medical facilities in Italy (see page 154). The Australian Medicare system also has a reciprocal health-care agreement.

Vaccinations are not required, and Italy does not present any serious health worries. Be aware, though, that it can become extremely hot in summer and it is sensible to protect yourself against the effects of this. Wear a hat and sunblock whenever necessary, and ensure you keep well hydrated. Drink bottled water as opposed to tap water, and definitely avoid drinking from the city fountains. Most minor ailments can be diagnosed and treated at a pharmacy (*farmacia*), identified throughout the city by the green cross sign. However, if you take prescriptive drugs, make sure you bring an adequate supply, as well as a letter from your doctor or personal health record card.

To all intents and purposes, Bologna is a safe city where the usual level of urban common sense will be sufficient to get you around without incident. Unlike other Italian cities to the south, there are no serious problems with street theft, muggings or drugs. That said, the city is full of dark alleys and shadowy arcades, so take care when walking alone at night. If leaving a restaurant or club late at night it is usually best to take a taxi.

OPENING HOURS

Shop hours are usually 09.30–13.00 & 15.30–20.00 Monday to Saturday. Many shops, restaurants, museums and galleries are closed for at least two weeks in August, some for the entire month. Banks are open 08.30–13.30 and 14.30–15.30 on weekdays, closed on Saturday and Sunday.

🔺 *Children chase the pigeons in Palazzo Comunale*

TOILETS

If you must use public toilets, train and bus stations are the best options, although don't expect them to be spotless. Museums and galleries also have toilet facilities. Most cafés and restaurants have public facilities for patrons only, so you may have to buy a drink in order to use them.

In some cases an attendant doles out *carta* (toilet paper) and expects a small tip in return. In Italy in general toilets run the gamut from clean and modern to a hole in the floor, so it's advisable to carry packets of sanitary wipes with you at all times.

CHILDREN

The Bolognese, like most Italians, love children, and are happy to cater for them in all manner of ways. As far as food goes, you will not go wrong with all the pasta choices, as well as pizza and, of course, ice cream. Restaurant chefs are usually very willing to prepare half portions of any dish.

To a child, all the churches, museums and libraries of Bologna and the surrounding towns can be boring, but the excellent book *Bologna for Kids*, with pages and pages of things to do and look for as they visit each church or museum, will keep them entertained. It's available from the tourist office (see page 151).

COMMUNICATIONS
Internet

The main Internet cafés in the city are in the public library at Piazza Nettuno 3 and Via de Chiara 5, near Piazza San Stefano. Under Italy's anti-terrorism legislation, photo ID is now required before you can use the Internet.

TELEPHONING ITALY

To phone Italy from abroad, dial the access code 00 from the UK, Ireland and New Zealand, 011 from the USA and Canada, 0011 from Australia, followed by the code for Italy 39, then the local number, including the full area code, which is 051 for Bologna.

TELEPHONING ABROAD

UK and Northern Ireland international access code 0044 + area code

Republic of Ireland international access code 00353 + area code

USA & Canada international access code 001 + area code

Australia international access code 0061 + area code

New Zealand international access code 0064 + area code

Phone

In Italy mobile phones work on the GSM European standard. Before you leave home make sure you have made the necessary roaming arrangements with your mobile phone company. UK, New Zealand and Australian mobile phones will work in Italy, but US and Canadian mobile phones may not. If you plan to stay in Italy for an extended period, or if you travel to Italy often, it may be worth purchasing an Italian SIM card for your mobile (visit any TIM or Vodafone mobile phone store for options). SIM cards normally cost between €5 and €10 and you'll need to show your passport when you make your purchase.

Post

The city's main post office is on the northern side of Piazza Minghetti, and is open 08.15–18.30 Monday to Friday and 08.15–13.00 Saturday.

The hours of business for smaller offices are 08.30–13.30 Monday to Saturday. Italy's postal reputation is not high, so expect mail to take a little longer to reach the destination than it would from other European countries.

ELECTRICITY

Italy functions on a 220V mains supply. Travellers from the UK and USA will need adaptors as Italian sockets are for plugs with two round pins. It is best to purchase an adaptor before leaving home, as they are much more expensive in Bologna.

TRAVELLERS WITH DISABILITIES

In general Italy is still behind in catering for the disabled, but Bologna is better than most Italian cities. Contact an agency before departure for more details, such as **Accessible Italy** (Ⓦ www.accessibleitaly.com) or **Vacanze Serene** (Ⓣ 800 271 027).

Other useful organisations to consult before your travels include: **RADAR**, the principal UK forum for people with disabilities. Ⓐ 12 City Forum, 250 City Road, London EC1V 8AF Ⓣ (020) 7250 3222 Ⓦ www.radar.org.uk

SATH (Society for Accessible Travel & Hospitality) advises US-based travellers with disabilities. Ⓐ 347 Fifth Ave, Suite 605, New York, NY 10016 Ⓣ (212) 447 7284 Ⓦ www.sath.org

TOURIST INFORMATION

Bologna's main IAT tourist office is located under the Palazzo Podestà at Piazza Maggiore. It provides more free maps and leaflets than you could possibly need. Within the same building is the Emporio della Cultura, which sells books, souvenirs and tickets for various events. Also here is the CST (Hotel Reservation Centre).

There are tourist kiosks, too, at the railway station and the Arrivals terminal at the airport.

Bologna IAT Tourist Office @ Piazza Maggiore 1 ❶ 051 239 660 ❶ 09.30–19.30 daily ⓝ Bus: 11, 13, 14, 17, 18, 19, 20, 25, 27, 29, 30, 86, A, B, Aerobus

CST ❶ 800 856 065 ⓦ www.cst.bo.it

BACKGROUND READING

Back to Bologna by Michael Dibdin. An enjoyable mystery that cleverly evokes the city vibe.

Giorgio Morandi: The Art of Silence by J Abramowicz. A beautifully illustrated journey through the works of the city's most famous artistic son.

⬥ *Mosaic in Ravenna's Church of San Vitale*

Emergencies

The following are emergency free-call numbers:
Ambulance (*Ambulanza*) ⓘ 118
Fire (*Vigili del Fuoco*) ⓘ 115
Police (*Polizia*, English-speaking helpline) ⓘ 112

Additional useful numbers:
Car breakdown ⓘ 116

Lost or stolen credit cards:
American Express ⓘ 06 72282
American Express Gold Card ⓘ 800 874 333
Diners Club ⓘ 800 864064
Eurocard, MasterCard, VISA ⓘ 800 018548

MEDICAL SERVICES
Accident and emergency
By law, all hospital accident and emergency rooms must treat all emergency cases for free. If you need urgent medical care, go to the *pronto soccorso* (casualty department). All the hospitals listed below offer 24-hour casualty services.

Hospitals
Ospedale Bellaria ⓐ Via Altura 3 ⓘ 622 5111 Ⓝ Bus: 36, 90
Ospedale Maggiore ⓐ Largo Nigrisoli 2 ⓘ 647 8111 Ⓝ Bus: 13, 19, 35, 38, 39, 81, 86, 87, 91, 92, 93, Aerobus
Ospedale Santa Orsola-Malpighi The city's main hospital.
ⓐ Via Massarenti 9, east of the city ⓘ 6363 111 Ⓝ Bus: 14, 19, 25, 27, 32, 33, 36, 89, 94, 99

◆ *Nifty mode of transport for police in Bologna*

PRACTICAL INFORMATION

EMERGENCY PHRASES

Help!	**Fire!**	**Stop!**
Aiuto!	Fuoco!	Fermi!
Ahyootoh!	*Fwohkoh!*	*Fehrmee!*

Call an ambulance/a doctor/the police/the fire service!
Chiami un'ambulanza/un medico/la polizia/i pompieri!
Kyahmee oon ahmboolahntsa/oon mehdeecoh/
lah pohleetseeyah/ee pohmpyehree!

Dentists
Contact the hospital (see page 152) or look in the *Pagine Gialle*
(*Yellow Pages*) under *Dentisti*.

Doctors
EU nationals with a European Health Insurance Card (EHIC)
can consult a national health service doctor free of charge, with any
drugs prescribed bought at chemists at prices set by the Health
Ministry. Tests and outpatient treatment are charged at fixed rates
also. Non-EU nationals who consult a health service doctor will be
charged a fee at the doctor's discretion, so make sure you have
adequate health insurance.

Opticians
Replacement lenses can usually be fitted overnight, and most
opticians will replace a missing screw or make adjustments on
the spot. See also *Ottica* in the *Pagine Gialle* (*Yellow Pages*).

Pharmacies

Farmacie (pharmacies) are identified by a green cross. Italian pharmacists are well qualified to give informal medical advice as well as dispense prescriptions. Make sure you know the generic as well as the brand name of your regular medicines, as they may be sold under a different name in Italy.

There is a large 24-hour pharmacy in the Piazza Maggiore, the **Farmacia Comunale**. If it's closed, a list on the door has details of the rotation of open pharmacies. 🄰 Piazza Maggiore 6 🛈 239 690 🄽 Bus: 11, 20, 29, 30

For an emergency pharmacist or for late-night delivery of medication, call the **Farmaco Pronto** 🛈 800 218 489

EMBASSIES & CONSULATES

There are no embassies in Bologna itself – the nearest main embassies are in Rome. Bologna does, however, at least have the **South African consulate** (🄰 Via Saragozza 12 🛈 331 306).

Embassies in Rome

Australia 🄰 Via Antonio Bosio 5, Rome 🛈 06 852 721 🄦 www.italy.embassy.gov.au

Canada 🄰 Via Zara 30, Rome 🛈 06 854 441 🄦 www.canada.it

Ireland 🄰 Piazza di Campitelli 3, Rome 🛈 06 697 9121

New Zealand 🄰 Via Zara 28, Rome 🛈 06 441 7171 🄦 www.nzembassy.com

United Kingdom 🄰 Via XX Settembre 80, Rome 🛈 06 4220 0001 (in emergency outside of office hours 🛈 06 4220 2603) 🄦 www.ukinitaly.fco.gov.uk

United States 🄰 Via Vittorio Veneto 121, Rome 🛈 06 46741 🄦 http://rome.usembassy.gov

ACKNOWLEDGEMENTS & FEEDBACK

ACKNOWLEDGEMENTS

The publishers would like to thank the following individuals and organisations for supplying their copyright photographs for this book: Patrik Axelsson, page 153; Bologna Turismo, pages 19, 23, 87 & 99; Bologna Turismo/Alessandro Salomoni, page 67; Centro Turistico Città di Bologna, page 41; Corrado, page 82; Dreamstime (Timurk, pages 42–3); Fototeca ENIT (Vito Arcomano page 109); Hotel Arcoveggio, page 38; istockphoto (bemotto, page 5; Giorgio Magini, page 105; StockCube, page 102; vertuio, page 110; Richard Waters, page 61); Paolo Margari, page 139; Pictures Colour Library, pages 31, 113; Timothy Sewter, page 70; Tourist Information Office, Ferrara, page 15 ; Teatro Comunale Bologna, page 90; World Pictures, pages 51 & 69; Barbara Rogers, all others.

Project Editor: Jennifer Jahn
Layout: Paul Queripel
Proofreaders: Caroline Hunt & Jan McCann

Send your thoughts to
books@thomascook.com

- Found a great bar, club, shop or must-see sight that we don't feature?
- Like to tip us off about any information that needs a little updating?
- Want to tell us what you love about this handy little guidebook and more importantly how we can make it even handier?

Then here's your chance to tell all! Send us ideas, discoveries and recommendations today and then look out for your valuable input in the next edition of this title.

Email the above address (stating the title) or write to:
pocket guides Series Editor, Thomas Cook Publishing, PO Box 227, Coningsby Road, Peterborough PE3 8SB, UK.

WHAT'S IN YOUR GUIDEBOOK?

Independent authors Impartial up-to-date information from our travel experts who meticulously source local knowledge.

Experience Thomas Cook's 165 years in the travel industry and guidebook publishing enriches every word with expertise you can trust.

Travel know-how Thomas Cook has thousands of staff working around the globe, all living and breathing travel.

Editors Travel-publishing professionals, pulling everything together to craft a perfect blend of words, pictures, maps and design.

You, the traveller We deliver a practical, no-nonsense approach to information, geared to how you really use it.

Useful phrases

English	Italian	Approx pronunciation
BASICS		
Yes	Sì	*See*
No	No	*Noh*
Please	Per favore	*Pehr fahvohreh*
Thank you	Grazie	*Grahtsyeh*
Hello	Buongiorno/Ciao	*Bwonjohrnoh/Chow*
Goodbye	Arrivederci/Ciao	*Ahreevehderchee/Chow*
Excuse me	Scusi	*Skoozee*
Sorry	Mi dispiace	*Mee deespyahcheh*
That's okay	Va bene	*Vah behneh*
I don't speak Italian	Non parlo italiano	*Non pahrloh eetahlyahnoh*
Do you speak English?	Parla inglese?	*Pahrlah eenglehzeh?*
Good morning	Buongiorno	*Bwonjohrnoh*
Good afternoon	Buon pomeriggio	*Bwon pohmehreejoh*
Good evening	Buona sera	*Bwonah sehrah*
Goodnight	Buona notte	*Bwonah nohteh*
My name is ...	Mi chiamo ...	*Mee kyahmoh ...*
NUMBERS		
One	Uno	*Oonoh*
Two	Due	*Dooeh*
Three	Tre	*Treh*
Four	Quattro	*Kwahttroh*
Five	Cinque	*Cheenkweh*
Six	Sei	*Say*
Seven	Sette	*Sehteh*
Eight	Otto	*Ohtoh*
Nine	Nove	*Nohveh*
Ten	Dieci	*Dyehchee*
Twenty	Venti	*Ventee*
Fifty	Cinquanta	*Cheenkwahntah*
One hundred	Cento	*Chentoh*
SIGNS & NOTICES		
Airport	Aeroporto	*Ahehrohpohrtoh*
Railway station	Stazione ferroviaria	*Statsyoneh fehrohveeahreeyah*
Platform	Binario	*Beenahreeyoh*
Smoking/non-smoking	Fumatori/non fumatori	*Foomahtohree/non foomahtohree*
Toilets	Bagni	*Bahnyee*
Ladies/Gentlemen	Signore/Signori	*Seenyoreh/Seenyohree*
Subway	Metropolitana	*Mehtrohpohleetahnah*